CADOGAN CHESS BOOKS

Danger in Chess

CADOGAN CHESS SERIES

Chief Adviser: Garry Kasparov
Editor: Andrew Kinsman

Other CADOGAN CHESS titles for the club and tournament player include:

ELIE AGUR
Bobby Fischer: His Approach to Chess

LEV ALBURT
Test and Improve Your Chess

YURI AVERBAKH
Chess Endings: Essential Knowledge

AMATZIA AVNI
Creative Chess

MICHAEL BASMAN
The New St. George

JULIAN HODGSON
The Chess Traveller's Quiz Book

GARRY KASPAROV
The Test of Time

DANIEL KING
How Good is Your Chess?

DANIEL KOPEC et al
Mastering Chess

EDMAR MEDNIS
How To Be a Complete Tournament Player

MIHAI SUBA
Dynamic Chess Strategy

SIMON WEBB
Chess for Tigers

For a complete catalogue of CADOGAN CHESS books (which includes the Pergamon Chess and Maxwell Macmillan Chess lists), please write to: Cadogan Books PLC, Letts House, Parkgate Road, London SW11 4NQ
Tel: 071-738 1961   Fax: 071-924 5491

Danger in Chess

by

Amatzia Avni

CADOGAN CHESS
LONDON, NEW YORK

CADOGAN BOOKS
DISTRIBUTION

UK/EUROPE/AUSTRALASIA/ASIA/AFRICA
Distribution: Grantham Book Services Ltd, Isaac Newton Way, Alma Park Industrial Estate, Grantham, Lincs NG31 9SD.
Tel: (0476) 67421;   Fax: (0476) 590223.

USA/CANADA/LATIN AMERICA/JAPAN
Distribution: Macmillan Distribution Center, Front and Brown Streets, Riverside, New Jersey 08075, USA.
Tel: (609) 461 6500;   Fax: (609) 764 9122.

First published 1994 by Cadogan Books PLC, Letts House, Parkgate Road, London SW11 4NQ

British Library Cataloguing-in-Publication Data
A CIP catalogue record for this book is available from the British Library

ISBN 1-85744-057-9

Cover design by Mark Levitt
Typesetting by Ann Park
Printed in Great Britain by BPCC Wheatons Ltd, Exeter

Contents

Acknowledgements

I'd like to take the opportunity to thank several people who gave me assistance in bringing this book to light: *Ilan Manor* and *Yochanan Afek* for some analytical help; my editors *Andrew Kinsman* and *Graham Hillyard* for making the book's language more fluent and readable; *Raaphy Persitz* who, as always, was supportive and encouraging towards my chess writing; and *Amiram Hayden* for technical advice.

The book is dedicated with love to my family: *Naama, Youval, Ohad* and *Yael*.

Amatzia Avni, November 1993
Ramat-Ilan, Israel

Symbols and Abbreviations

W	White to move	!?	Interesting move
B	Black to move	?!	Dubious move
0-0	Castles kingside	=	Equal position
0-0-0	Castles queenside	±	Advantage to White
e.p.	En passant	∓	Advantage to Black
x	Captures	±±	Winning for White
+	Check	∓∓	Winning for Black
!	Good move	Ch.	Championship
!!	Brilliant move	Ol.	Olympiad
?	Bad move	corr.	Correspondence
??	Blunder	izt	Interzonal

Introduction

The rules of chess do not keep score of accumulated interim results.

A player can build up a sizeable advantage over his (or her) opponent and keep it during most stages of the contest; but a few seconds lack of attention can squander all his hard work. In chess no one counts "advantages" or "winning positions"; only the final result matters. Consequently a mistake in chess can be of greater significance than in games where interim results do count, like football, basketball, table-tennis, etc.

In these games a player or a team leading by a considerable margin may allow themselves the luxury of grave errors; at worst it will narrow the difference. On the other hand, bad blunders in chess can nullify all former achievements, even turn the tables. Any (chess) move can be critical, any decision may determine the outcome of the whole battle.

Bearing in mind the significance of chess mistakes, it could be argued that a chessplayer is required to display a high and constant level of concentration, in comparison with a competitor in other games or pursuits. He cannot permit himself to rest on his laurels during the game; he should be tense like a spring, always alert and attentive.

The trouble is that this demand is not realistic; people are unable to maintain a high attention level for prolonged periods. They tire, their minds wander and watchfulness decreases. You can verify this assertion by observing the behaviour of drivers on the road, or frontier guards on sentry duty. Clearly both have strong motivation to maintain maximum attention – any diminution of watchfuless can cost a life, possibly their own. Do they succeed in staying fully alert and watchful for many hours? Hardly.

Back to chess. To be honest, the alertness of chessplayers (including the very best) is not constant. Sometimes we relax, at other times we day-dream and let our thoughts wander (even in our own thinking time). Sometimes we get distracted by things that have nothing to do with chess. And only for part of the time that our own clock is ticking do we put all our efforts into evaluating and calculating the various possibilities on the board.

A glance around the tournament hall lends support to the hypothesis that the competitors switch from rest to alertness, from wandering with dreamy eyes to energetic investigation of the board situation. Contrary to what non-players believe, chessplayers do find time for idle dreams and fleeting thoughts.

So far we have made two main points, which are of a contradictory character. First, that on account of the game's rules the player is obliged to display continued high-level vigilance; and secondly, that being human, this task is beyond his reach.

The question is: How do chessplayers manage to bridge the gulf between what they can do and what they should do? To be more specific: How do they identify when they are free to "dream" and when they must mobilise all their resources and capabilities? How do they succeed in classifying (competently) the position on the board as "safe" or "dangerous" for them?

In a way that is not totally clear, stronger players manage somehow to "know" (without concrete analysis of variations) when they can move quickly and when, on the other hand, they must take the utmost care, plunge into deep thought and re-examine the accuracy of former assessments.

Our wonder and admiration at this skill of competent players may be even greater if we return to the comparison of chess with other sports. In soccer, a goalkeeper seeing five forwards rushing towards him with the ball cannot misinterpret their intention. In a long-distance race, a runner noticing the spectators getting up and roaring, grasps immediately that something is happening. At tennis, a situation of set point makes it clear to the protagonists that a critical moment has arrived.

All these signals are absent in chess. The issue is frequently resolved not by a direct attack against the king. Hence, the player may face difficulties in recognising that an aggressive action is taking place against him. Spectators – if present at all – are not allowed to utter a sound, according to the regulations. Finally, there being no limit on the length of a game (at least not in "serious" tournaments), no critical situation is *a priori* defined as such. Moreover, a chess game is played from the beginning to the end with the competitors in a state of comparative uncertainty. A player almost never knows his situation during the game; he only assumes. His state is therefore much more difficult than that of a swimmer, who knows at least if he is in the lead or not, or that of the sharpshooter, who gets continual feedback after every shot.

In life most people prefer to purchase articles that have signals which will act as warning signs in case of any failure or breakdown. If something is wrong, the computer will flash an error. A red light will come on in a malfunctioning car; bad smell or taste will signify spoiled food, and a smoke detector will produce an alarm sound in the event of a fire.

And in chess?

Well, square a1 is not going to flicker as a warning sign. The hostile knight will not change its colour. Our opponent will not alert us by shouting in our ears "Beware!".

And with all that, in spite of a complete lack of outside aids, strong chessplayers do receive (or produce) warning signals and can interpret them correctly. Finding an answer to the question, "How do they do it?", is important and contains significant implications.

If we were able to define and characterise those signals, and pin-point situations liable to cause failures in the alarm system, and if we could determine what kind of positions contain the probability of danger, then we would be able to develop and sharpen this instinct. We would establish this "feeling for danger" as an object of study of equal importance to, for instance, "coping with an isolated pawn" or "when to exchange pieces". One could derive great practical use from it. The characterisation of typical positions where there is a high probability of the danger-instinct failing might, by a player's very awareness of these archetypes, lessen such slips.

Conversely, a better understanding of the signals that broadcast danger may also help us to lull the adversary's feelings of danger, by implementing masking tactics of disguise and deception.

These are the subjects of the present book.

In the absence of serious research data, the following will reflect more the author's thoughts, ideas and theories than proven, valid facts.

It is to be hoped that further works on this issue will enlighten us more, thus broadening our understanding.

1 The Sense of Danger – Its Meaning and Importance

In the chess literature of recent decades there are references to what is called a sense of danger. The purpose of this sense is: "to be aware of impending danger in time, and to avoid it" – Alexander Kotov.[1] This probably means that certain signs – perhaps at a subconscious level – act as alarm signals for the chessplayer, indicating that he must raise his vigilance.

The usual indicators of control systems provide us with *feedbacks*, that is they pin-point something that has already gone wrong. Here we are dealing with signals whose aim is to provide us with *feed-forward*; to point out the probability of future failures. A feed-forward system "is a means of seeing problems as they develop and not looking back – always too late – to see why a planning target was missed."[2]

Drawing an analogy with real battle, here is "something" that distinguishes between routine and emergency, between a relatively peaceful situation and the outbreak of hostilities.

One example of a variable related to the sense of danger is correct timing:

"The player feels, for example, that the moment has come when delay will mean death, that it is exactly now and not later that he must begin the counterattack. . . This sense of of timing is manifested for instance in the feeling of danger, which is familiar to many players . . ." – Nikolai Krogius.[3]

Also, this sixth sense is related to the skill of "entering the opponent's mind". Annotating a game lost by Bobby Fischer, GM Edmar Mednis wrote: "White is dreaming of his attack, completely oblivious to the fact that it is Black who is doing the attacking!"[4]

Such a mistake stems from focusing too much on what we plan, while ignoring the other side's intentions. A developed sense of danger means orienting one's own thoughts towards perceiving the rival's train of thought.

As many authorities advise, it

is useful to put oneself in the opponent's place, to think from his point of view.

Descriptions of the sense of danger sometimes appear in connection with the terms "critical position" or "critical moment". For instance, British trainer John Littlewood writes:

"We have to learn to detect critical moments in play . . . In a real game situation we learn to develop, with practice, a sixth sense about such critical moments." [5]

Acquiring a developed sense of danger apparently helps us to spot critical moments in the game. The trouble is that both terms are rather vague, and leave the student wondering how to recognise critical moments, whatever that means, before they arrive.

The most detailed characterisation of the sense of danger and its working mechanism during a chess game is given by Mark Dvoretsky, widely regarded as the number one chess trainer in the former USSR:

"The opponent makes an apparently innocent move, but for some reason or another he rouses our vigilance and promptly we discover the cunning that is concealed. Another instance: We abandon serious consideration of a move that at first sight looked tempting, because we feel that there must be a refutation. Or: the variations that we work out are all to our advantage, but a "feeling for danger" forces us to check and recheck repeatedly; and we discover an error somewhere in the calculation.

"Clearly in such a situation there is a connection between pure chess information . . . and psychologically influenced decisions." [6]

It is quite common for players to treat this mysterious intuitive sense as something very realistic/ materialistic, and to attribute errors in games to "failures" of the danger-detector. "The reason for my awful oversight was that over-confidence sapped my sense of danger," writes Kotov. [7]

Let's have a look at a few examples that demonstrate the importance of a danger instinct.

1   W

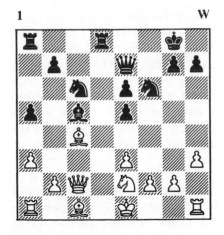

The preceding diagram is a modified version of a position played in 1982 between two Israeli junior players.

A brief study of the diagram brings out the weakness of Black's isolated and doubled e-pawns. Asked to choose a White move, the majority of strong players would probably single out 1 0-0.

Although 1 ♗xe6+ wins a pawn, experienced tournament players would not seriously contemplate this move. They would rule out the possibility on the grounds that "it does not smell good" to grab pawns before completing development, and would reach a decision without concrete calculation.

In fact, a refutation of 1 ♗xe6+ does exist:

1	...	♕xe6
2	♕xc5	♕b3!!

Surprisingly, White now cannot save himself from heavy losses: 3 0-0 ♘e4 ∓∓, or 3 ♘c3 ♘e4! (still!) 4 ♕b5 ♖d1+.

The point, however, is that a White player can reach the right conclusion on the basis of his awareness of danger, without the necessity for precise analysis.

Diagram 2 presents a further demonstration of the common use of the "feeling for danger".

Shvidler-Stisis
2 Ramat Hasharon 1989   **W**

A sharp-eyed player would notice the possibility 1 ♗xe4+. A concrete calculation has a lot to say for this move: 1 ... ♖xe4+!? 2 ♖xe4 ♘xe4 3 d7; or 1 ... ♘xe4? 2 ♖d5+ ♔f6 4 d7 are in White's favour.

Still, self-pinning the white bishop whilst the rook is also under attack looks very suspect. This feeling prompted IM Shvidler to recheck the variations, and his doubts were soon verified: 1 ♗xe4+? actually loses to 1 ... ♔e6!!, temporarily unpinning, but 2 ♖d2 ♔d7 renews the pin with decisive effect.

Usually it is not at all easy to spot the critical moment, or identify an approaching danger. Diagram 3 shows an innocent-looking position in which Black should apparently feel safe, having neither structural deficiencies nor any obvious reason to worry about his king's position.

Quinones-Silva
3   Tel Aviv Ol. 1964   B

However, in the actual game Black went rapidly downhill:

1	...	$\pounds$xf3
2	$\rlap{\text{\Wunderlined}}$xf3	$\textcircled{2}$d7
3	Ξed1	$\textcircled{2}$b6
4	$\rlap{\text{\W}}$g4	$\rlap{\text{\W}}$c6
5	$\pounds$e7	Ξfe8
6	Ξd6	$\rlap{\text{\W}}$b7
7	$\pounds$f6	g6
8	Ξad1	**Resigns**

What were Black's mistakes? The position after 5 $\pounds$e7 is won for White, so we have to look for improvements at earlier stages. One commentator[8] blamed 1 ... $\pounds$xf3, suggesting 1 ... Ξfd8, but this is surely wrong, on account of 2 Ξxa6! [and if 2 ... $\textcircled{2}$xe4 then 3 $\pounds$h4 f5 4 Ξxa8 Ξxa8 5 $\rlap{\text{\W}}$d7 – *Ed.*].

2 ... $\textcircled{2}$e8 with the intention of 3 ... $\textcircled{2}$c7, 4 ... $\textcircled{2}$e6 looks better (e.g. 3 b4 $\rlap{\text{\W}}$c7 with 4 ... f6 to regroup), as does 4 ... $\textcircled{2}$h8. But it seems that Black's biggest error was that he was not aware that he was in danger! That is, until it was too late to do something about it.

Even more confusing is the next diagram.

Keres-Penrose
4   Hastings 1958   W

Black's queen and two knights appear to be a threatening force, while White also has to reckon with an advance of the h4 pawn;
Strangely, and contrary to first impressions, it is White who holds the initiative:

1	$\pounds$xf4	$\textcircled{2}$xf4
2	$\textcircled{2}$e3!	h3

2 ... $\oplus$h6!.

| 3 | $\textcircled{2}$g4! | |

Now, if 3 ... hxg2 (crushing?) 4 ♕d7+ ♔g8 5 ♕e8+ ♔g7 6 ♕e7+ and White is the first to deliver mate!

So Black had to settle for an ending, but without success:

3	...	♕xg2+
4	♕xg2	♘xg2
5	♘xe5	♘e3
6	c3	♔g7
7	♔h2	♔f6
8	♘d3	b6
9	♔xh3	c5
10	♔g3	c4
11	♔f2!	♘d1+
12	♔e2	♘xc3+
13	bxc3	cxd3+
14	♔xd3	♔e5
15	a5	g5
16	axb6	axb6
17	♔e3	**Resigns**

Chessplayers may fail to recognise a danger even long after it has landed on the board, screaming "Here I am!".

Veteran IM J.Porath recalls the following incident:

(diagram 5)

"White's only chance is to 'run' with his king to the centre. Analysing the adjourned position, I came to the conclusion that the king is too slow, and my only hope was that my adversary would play imprecisely and would fail to discern a latent saving possibility."

Porath-Walther
Havana Ol. 1966   **W**

5

The game continued:

1	♔e4	a2
2	♗xa2	♘xa2
3	f5	♔g7?

3 ... ♔g5! wins.

4	♔e5	♔f7
5	f6	♘c3
6	♔f5	

"Here my opponent continued with the expression of a winner 6 ... ♘d5 7 ♔g5 ♘xf6" – says Porath – "and it was only after 8 ♔h6! that he realised that he was in one of the no-win positions of a knight and pawn vs pawn!"[9] **Draw**.

True, it is not always so baffling. In certain positions the warning signals are evident.

Thiman-Felbecker
corr. 1968

6   W

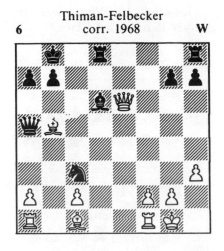

6	g3	♛f3+
7	♔h2	♛c6
8	♛xg7	♖f8
9	♖e3?	♘e4
10	♛xh7	♘d2
11	♔g1	♘xf1
12	♔xf1	♝c5

And in view of the continuation
13 ♛g7 ♖d8 **White resigned**.

However, frequently a certain
measure of intuition is required to
recognise the looming danger.

Alekhine-Lasker
Zürich 1934

7   B

Instead of the solid 1 ♝d3
White chose **1 ♝d2?!** which was
strongly countered by **1 ... ♛b6!**
getting out of the pin and threatening to win the queen by discovered
check. Such a nasty surprise
would be enough to wake up most
players, but White remained asleep,
falling for the same trick once
more!

2 ♝d7?

2 ♝c4.

2	...	♖xd7!
3	♛xd7	♛d4!

The threat of discovered check,
formerly appearing on a rank,
now re-emerges on a file. Probably
White should now have given up
his queen (4 ♝xc3 ♝h2+ 5 ♔xh2).

4	♔h1?	♛xd2
5	♖ae1	♛f4

Black was feeling confident
enough in this position to play **1
... ♛b6?**, intending to challenge
control of the d-file. Had he
played 1 ... g6 he would have
obtained a satisfactory position,
but the queen sortie enabled the
great attacking player of the
white pieces to launch a powerful
offensive:

| 2 | ♕d6! | ♘ed7 |

2 ... ♘g6? 3 ♘h6+.

3	♖fd1	♖ad8
4	♕g3	g6
5	♕g5!	♔h8
6	♘d6	♔g7
7	e4	♘g8
8	♖d3	f6

8 ... h6 9 ♘f5+ ♔h7 10 ♘xh6 f6 11 ♘f5!! brings a similar finish.

| 9 | ♘f5+ | ♔h8 |
| 10 | ♕xg6! | Resigns |

Hug-Biyiasas
8   Haifa Ol. 1976   B

In this position too Black has, apparently, no cause to feel uneasy. True, White intends to gain the upper hand with 2 ♘g5, but this positional threat can be parried, for instance, by **1 ... ♗f6**.

That is how Black played. The rationale is correct, but the chosen move is a grave error.

Question 1: What was the danger that eluded Black?

Tukmakov-Karpov
9   Leningrad izt 1973   B

White is a whole exchange behind, with no compensation whatsoever. His last move, 1 ♔g1-f1, seems pointless. The rook under attack has three respectable options: d2, b2 and e4. They all look good enough to clinch the win.

Question 2: Are they?

In the course of a chess battle a player wavers. Is everything going well? Is my position strong? Will I be able to carry out my plans?

The answers to these questions are compared with hints the player gets from various sources. Signals may originate from inner feelings, or from the opponent's behaviour, or from factors such as the conduct of spectators. But first and foremost, the player continually tests what he thinks and feels against what his evaluation and analysis of the board situation tell him. A player builds for himself, mostly unknowingly, a system of signals whose aim is to broadcast to him the presence of dangers, real or potential. The system forms, grows and stabilises with accumulated experience.

The idea is that *each* signal, independently, can press the 'alarm' button, thus calling for concrete calculation of variations on top of general strategic reasoning.

It must be pointed out that signals suggest the *possibility* of a dangerous situation, but do not constitute a testimony of its *existence.*

In chess, it is never possible to prove in advance that something will occur. Still, to own a good sense of danger is undoubtedly a valuable asset.

Let us observe the danger-signal system at work.

2   Obvious Dangers

We have already observed that many of the dangers awaiting a player during a game are not easy to foresee. Either the danger is concealed – the player is unaware of the risk involved – or he fails to interpret correctly the chess and psychological data.

However, before we delve into this matter, let us briefly review some well-known dangerous situations. These are positions that, by the very process of learning the game's rules and principles, we have already come to recognise as inherently risky.

I. Leaving the king with insufficient support from other pieces

(diagram 10)

1	♕c2?!	0-0
2	♘fd2?	

The natural follow-up to his previous move, but removing the king's knight from its defensive duties is brilliantly refuted:

2	...	♘xf2!
3	♔xf2	

Duncan-Alperovitch
10   Tel Aviv 1990   **W**

If 3 ♖xe7 then 3 ... ♘xd3 is simple and strong. 3 ... ♗d1 is less convincing on account of 4 ♕xd1 ♘xd1 5 ♖e1! collecting a third piece for the queen.

3	...	♗h4+
4	g3	f4!
5	♔g2	fxg3
6	hxg3	♗h3+!
7	♔xh3	♗xg3

The white monarch is completely naked now, waiting for his execution . . .

8	♗xh7+	♔h8

12

9	♘f3	♖xf3
10	♖h1	♗f4+
11	♔g2	♕g5+!

Very impressive.

12	♔xf3	♕g3+
13	♔e2	♕g2+
14	♔e1	♕xh1+
15	♔f2	

And now the simplest was 15 ...
♖f8. **Black won.**

Golovko-Karasev
11   USSR 1965   W

| 1 | ♕xa7 |

Grabbing this distant pawn is
playable, but Black now develops
a certain initiative, which demands
some careful play on White's
part.

1	...	♕b4
2	♗f3	♖c8
3	d6	

It was better to return the

queen to participate in the defence,
by 3 ♕e3.

| 3 | ... | ♗a4! |
| 4 | ♕xb7? | |

But this is really careless. It was
essential to play 4 d7 ♖d8 5 ♕d4,
e.g. 5 ... ♕a5 6 ♕d5! ♕b6 7 ♕d4.

| 4 | ... | ♗c2+! |
| 5 | ♔a1 | |

5 ♔c1? ♗f5+.

| 5 | ... | ♗xd1 |
| 6 | ♕xe7+ | |

What else? 6 ♕xc8? ♗xf3 7
♕e6 ♕d2! 8 ♕xe7+ ♔h6 is
hopeless.

6	...	♔h6
7	♕e3+	g5
8	♗xd1	♕e1!
White resigns		

9 ♕h3+ ♔g7 10 ♕d7+ ♔g6 and
the checks are over.

II. Weakness of the eighth rank

(diagram 12)

There are several advantages for
Black in this position: a queenside
pawn majority, strong outposts
for his heavy pieces, a weak and
blockaded white d-pawn. But his
single disadvantage – no 'luft' for
his king – brings his demise.

| 1 | ♖c2! | ♕xd4 |

Lepek-Koonen
12   1962   W

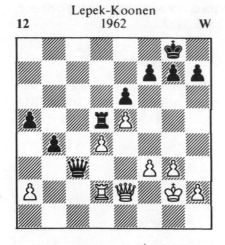

2	♖c4!	♕b6
3	♖c8+	♖d8
4	♕b5!	

Or 4 ♕e3!.

Black resigned

III. Entering a lasting pin

Gomes-Neto
13   Rio de Janeiro 1942   B

White is in dire straits, not because he is pinned along the d1-h5 diagonal, but because it is difficult to break this pin. He would need some tempi (♘a3-b1-d2, or c3, ♖ad1, d4, ♕e3) to ease his situation. Meanwhile Black can prepare his onslaught.

1	...	♖g8!!

With the magnificent idea of 2 ... ♘h4+! 3 gxh4 g5!. White is defenceless.

2	c3

2 ♘b1 ♘h4+! 3 gxh4 g5 4 ♘1d2 will fail to 4 ... g4!.

2	...	♘h4+!
3	gxh4	g5
4	♖g1	♗xf3+
5	♕xf3	gxh4+

White resigns

IV. Capturing "poisoned" pawns

(diagram 14)

Black is a pawn up and 1 ... ♗e7 would put him in an advantageous position. It is remarkable that of all people, it was the solid and careful future world champion Botvinnik who chose the insane 1 ... ♘xe3 2 ♗xe3 ♕xc3?? after which White developed an irresistible attack along the open b- and c-files.

Kan-Botvinnik
14   Moscow 1935   **B**

The rest was:

3	♖fc1	♕a5
4	♕c2!	c6

He must weaken his pawn formation, for if 4 ... ♖d7 then 5 ♗d2 ♕a3 6 ♖b3 followed by 7 ♖1b1.

5	♗d2	♕c7
6	♕a4	

With the double threat of 7 ♗xa6 and 7 ♗a5.

6	...	♖d7
7	♗xa6	Resigns

Another example of helping the opponent with his attack is the following diagram.

1 ♕xc5 is forced. The continuation chosen by 15-year-old Kasparov is suicidal:

Kasparov–Sideif-Zade
15   USSR 1978   **W**

1	♕a8+?	♔d7
2	♗h3+	f5
3	♕xb7	♕c2+
4	♔a1	♗d6

Now that the black rooks are united, ready to occupy the a- and b-files, White does not stand a chance.

5	♕d5

5 ♗c3 ♖b8 6 ♕d5 ♕xc3!.

5	...	♖a8
6	♗a5	

6 ♕xd4? ♖xa2+.

6	...	♕a4
7	b4	

Forced.

7	...	♖xa5!
8	bxa5	

8 ♕xa5 ♘b3+.

8	...	♘c2+
9	♔b2	♖b8+
10	♔c1	♘d4!
11	♔d2	♛b4+

White resigns

V. Placing pieces without escape-routes

Razvaliev-Kolikshtein
16   Tashkent 1972   B

1	...	♛h5?

1 ... ♝b4 was appropriate. Black's choice puts the queen in a vulnerable position.

2	h3	0-0
3	♔e2!!	

A stunning move which gains material.

3	...	e5
4	g4	♝xg4
5	hxg4	♛xg4
6	♛g1	♛e6

A piece down, Black naturally avoids exchanges, but now White develops a crushing attack.

7	♖xh7!	exd4+
8	♝e3!	♘xh7
9	♝xh7+	♔h8
10	♛h1	g6
11	♝xg6+	♔g7
12	♛h6+	♔f6
13	♝f5+!	**Resigns**

The preceding diagrams contained prominent danger signals. They had features that are widely known to imply risk, and chess manuals are crammed with warnings about the dangers involved.

Other situations, like performing 'sins' against the rules of development, letting an enemy rook occupy the seventh rank, or rushing one's moves during the adversary's time trouble, are also well-known to be dangerous.

Hardicsay-Adorjan
17   Hungary 1986   W

1 ♗b5

Simple and better was 1 ♗e2. White intends to prevent the freeing move ... c5, but he forgets to pay attention to his own position.

1 ... c6
2 ♗a4?

It was not too late to play 2 ♗e2.

2 ... ♗a6!
3 e4

After 3 ♗xc6? ♗f6 4 a4 b5 White will lose material, but now his king is stuck in the centre with no compensation at all.

3 ... ♘f6
4 ♘d2 ♛c7
5 f3? ♘d5!!
White resigns

Since preventing mate (6 ... ♗h4+) will cost him the queen.

Alas, not all dangers appear in such a clear-cut form. There are dangerous situations that are not so evident, which require a certain degree of wisdom (chess or otherwise) to spot and prevent before they materialise. These concealed dangers will be discussed in the following chapters.

Common Failures in the Sensing of Danger

The next three chapters are an attempt to outline various types of dangerous situation which are liable to catch out unsuspecting souls.

The situations are organised according to their characteristics:

Chapter 3 is about dangers that stem from the *opponent*, be it his identity (e.g. a woman player), his manners/behaviour, or his play (weak or incomprehensible).

Chapter 4 deals with dangers that are created by certain developments on the *chessboard*. It deals with such questions as what happens to a player who finds himself in a dominating position, handling an ending with very little material, making a series of mass exchanges, and more.

Chapter 5 covers chess dangers deriving from another source, the human *thought-process*, with its limitations: confusing right and wrong, the critical with the not so impৎrtant; tending to think for our side, while neglecting the other side's motives and goals; relaxing our concentration after achieving a success, etc.

By looking through the examples in these chapters the reader will develop a pretty good feeling for the types of situation in which the probability of a particular danger increases.

3   Common Failures in the Sensing of Danger: Opponent-Related Factors

I. When the opponent plays badly in the opening

Suppose you play against someone who makes some silly moves, right from the start. He sheds material, or plays not in accordance with development rules, or he makes apparently self-destructive moves . . . Most chess players, when faced with such an enemy, tend to relax and expect an early success. It is a human trait to count on consistency in behaviour; if our adversary played weakly until now, so we reason, he is likely to demonstrate the same low quality in the following phases of the game as well.

This line of thought is devoid of empirical justification. Our opponent may possess poor openings knowledge, but still be a strong middlegame player. Or he may have deliberately made early provocations to lead us to think that our victory is assured.

Whatever our impression about our rival's level of play, we must stay on guard!

18   Lowens-Stafford
USA 1950   **W**

The above position arose after the moves **1 e4 e5 2 ♘f3 ♘f6 3 ♘xe5 ♘c6? 4 ♘xc6 dxc6 5 e5 ♘e4**.

Black has given up a pawn for nothing, or so it seems. White can choose between a host of natural moves: 6 d4, 6 d3, 6 ♘c3, 6 ♗c4, 6 ♕f3, 6 c3, among others.

They all look safe and sound; but the impression is misleading. 6 ♗c4 is unnecessarily complicated, although probably playable: 6 ... ♘xf2? 7 ♕f3, or 6 ... ♕d4 7 ♕e2.

19

6 d4 c5 is also not the best. However, certainly not **6 d3??** (which occurred in the game) **6 ... ♗c5!** after which **White resigned**(!) since both 7 dxe4 ♗xf2+ and 7 ♗e3 ♗xe3 8 fxe3 ♛h4+ lead to defeat.

In the next example, White implemented a most peculiar opening scheme:

1	♘c3	c5
2	♖b1?	

If his first move could be regarded as "original", his second move is plain stupid. Black can now claim that he has already attained equality, but he must understand that if the enemy begins to play sensibly, then despite his bizarre opening White will not be worse.

2	...	♘f6
3	g3	d5
4	♗g2	e5
5	e4	

(diagram 19)

What would you do now? 5 ... d4, 5 ... ♗e6, 5 ... ♗g4, or 5 ... dxe4 all appear to be satisfactory for Black.

Question 3: Try to spot a concealed danger.

19   Twyble-Sugden
     Southend 1986   B

The next position arose after the following moves:

1	e4	c5
2	♘f3	e6
3	d3	♘c6
4	g3	g6
5	d4	

Rather unusual, but perfectly logical. The holes in Black's dark squares justify the loss of time involved in making the advance d2-d4 in two moves.

5	...	cxd4
6	♘xd4	♗g7?

He should have prevented White's next move with 6 ... a6.

7 ♘b5

An unpleasant situation for Black. Of course 7 ... d5 will be met by 8 exd5 exd5 9 ♛xd5.

7 ...   ♘f6?!

Black's last two moves seem to show a total disregard for his adversary's plans. Now the White player probably thought something like this: "Obviously 8 ♘d6+ leads to my advantage, but this guy plays so badly . . . isn't it time to finish him off?"

8 ♕d6 (??)

And wins?

8 ...   ♘xe4!!

Yes, but the winner is Black! After 9 ♘c7+ ♕xc7 10 ♕xc7 ♗e5! or 9 ♕f4 d5! 10 f3 e5 White is a pawn down with a ruined position.

The moves immediately prior to the next diagram have left White an exchange up.

Smyslov-Kasparov
21   USSR Team Ch. 1981   W

In his notes to the game[10] Kasparov refrains from calling this a "sacrifice", so it is possible that he simply miscalculated. Probably that is also what his opponent thought.

1 ♖d2

"White should probably have considered 1 d5," writes Kasparov, "but why return the exchange when there is no immediately apparent danger?"

1 ...   f5
2 ♖e1?!   ♕c8!
3 ♕c3?

3 e4 fxe4 4 ♖xe4 ♗g5 5 ♖e3! was equal, according to Kasparov.

3 ...   ♖f6
4 a3?

No one can afford to make

successive errors, playing against such a formidable enemy. Smyslov did not sense the seriousness of his position, otherwise he would have played 4 ♕d3 intending 5 e4!.

4	...	♕e8!
5	dxc5	♕h5
6	h4	

Black threatened 6 ... ♕xh2+. But now White's position is beyond salvation.

6	...	♕g4
7	♔h2	bxc5
8	♖h1	♖g6
9	♔g1	♗xh4
10	♕a5	h6

White resigns

II. When the opponent plays incomprehensibly

Sometimes the guy we are fighting against makes a move that appears at first to be pointless. It does not defend anything, nor does it attack a concrete target. It seems not to be connected with any plan . . .

In short, it is as if the enemy has just moved aimlessly . . . The natural reaction is to pass the verdict "rubbish" and to go on with our intended plan.

However, degrading our rival to a level of woodpusher is not particularly clever, to say the least. Perhaps he *does* have a point, one that is evading us . . .

"When your opponent makes a move which looks like an obvious blunder – especially if he is a pretty strong player – it is advisable to try to find out what he has overlooked" – GM Lev Alburt.[11]

Also, one should add, check twice to make sure that it is *he* who has overlooked something.

Annotating a losing blunder by the Swedish GM Ulf Andersson, who naively grabbed a pawn and was mated, GM Edmar Mednis enquired gently: "Shouldn't he have been suspicious of Black *voluntarily* placing the c-pawn *en prise*?"[12]

A more extreme case happens when our rival makes a move which seems to comply with our plans. Not only does he not try to prevent our schemes, he actually encourages them!

This is a clear reason for becoming suspicious.

(diagram 22)

White has advanced his d-pawn too far, and is now going to lose it (1 ... ♖fd8, and if necessary, 2 ... g5, 3 ... ♔g7, 4 ... ♘f7).

| 1 | ♖e1(!) | ♖fd8?? |

Black interpreted White's last as meaningless.

Middleton-Rubinstein
22   Barmen 1905   **W**

2   ♘xc6   ♚xe6
3   f4!

One presumes that it was quite a shock for Black to realise that he was now losing a piece! (3 ... cxf3 c.p. or 3 ... ♘ moves will be answered by 4 ♗c4 mate! **White won**.

Ljubojević-Nogueiras
23   Wijk aan Zee 1987   **W**

Black's last move was ... ♘c6-e5. Now a sensible answer was to castle, since he has no time to keep his bishop: 1 ♗e2? d3 or 1 ♗e4? ♗c4!. White, however, took Black's move as an oversight, and rushed to carry out the standard

1   ♗xh7+?   ♚xh7
2   ♕h5+   ♚g8
3   ♕xe5

It was only after

3   ...   ♖e8!

that he realised the catastrophe he brought upon himself. For the price of a mere pawn Black obtained a vehement attack.

4   ♕g3   ♗c4+
5   ♚d1   ♖c8
6   b3   ♗e2+
7   ♚c1   d3
8   c3   ♗h5
9   ♖a2   ♖e2
10   ♚b1

And now 10 ... ♕b6 11 ♕h3 ♖xc3! 12 ♗xc3 ♕xb3+ 13 ♗b2 ♕c2+ 14 ♚a1 d2 would have been the clearest. **Black won**.

(diagram 24)

1   ♗c4   ♕xe4?

Ex-world champion Karpov tortured his opponent for many moves, waiting for him to make a mistake; finally Black succumbed! He should have asked himself:

Karpov-M.Gurevich
24 Reggio Emilia 1991 W

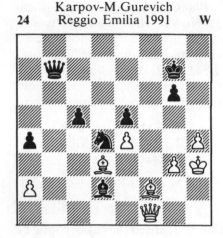

"Why does White give up his e4 pawn?" The correct move was 1 ... ♛d7+ with a tenable game.

2	♗xd4	exd4
3	♛f7+	♚h6
4	♛f8+	♚h5
5	♛h8+	♗h6
6	♛e5+!!	Resigns

III. When the opponent has an indifferent reputation

Most of us treat our opponents differently from one another. The stronger the opposition, the more seriously we tend to take it.

We put more effort into our preparation, accord the other side's moves greater respect, contemplate longer at our turn . . .

Against "patzers" we have a tendency to take things somewhat lightheartedly. Many players are guilty (although they probably would not admit it) of believing that their "weakie" rival will crack any minute, so they just have to "make some moves": the enemy's resignation being a matter of time.

In the good old days, the "willing victims" were easily identified. They included women, youngsters, oldies, players from underdeveloped countries, and chess computers.

Times have changed a little, though. The Polgar sisters, Indian star Anand, supercomputer "Deep Thought" – all these ought to have made the former views obsolete. However, it is not easy to abandon old habits, and many players have experienced major difficulties adapting to the new realities.

Playing against supposedly weak opposition, one tends to relax. This could precisely be the root of one's downfall. Especially when the pussycat turns out to be a tiger . . .

(diagram 25)

In the position below, playing against 12-year-old Judit Polgar, GM Pal Benko, former candidate for the world championship, blundered badly with

J.Polgar-Benko
25   New York 1988   B

Greenfeld-J.Polgar
26   Haifa 1989   W

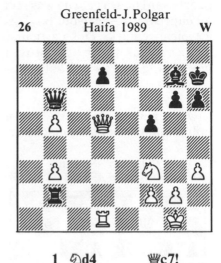

1 ...   ♘b4??

The girl answered

2 ♗xb6!

winning a pawn with the better
position, since 2 ... ♕xc4? is met
by 3 ♘a5.

Says Benko: "I don't believe I
would have made such a mistake
against an adult male opponent." [13]

One year later, the Israeli GM
Alon Greenfeld lost a superior
position to Judit, falling victim to
a beautiful trick (see diagram
26).

Commenting on this game,
Greenfeld said that he did not experience special problems, "though
it is possible that I was sub-
consciously influenced." [14]

1 ♘d4   ♕c7!
2 h4?

Completely missing the threat
contained in Black's last move.

2 ...   ♖d2!!

Astonishingly, White has no
way to prevent material loss.

3 ♖e1

Or 3 ♖xd2 ♕c1+ 4 ♔h2 ♕xd2
and the d4 knight is doomed.

3 ...   ♖xd4
4 ♕f7   ♖xh4
5 g3   ♖e4

And **Black won.**

A similar tendency, to underrate the enemy, may occur when
confronting a young male player.

"I was not quite ready to
believe he was as good as some

people said he was . . . he was still an unproven 15-year-old boy", is a typical remark. This particular quote is Benko's, the "unproven boy" being a certain Bobby Fischer.[15]

One tends to underrate not only humans, but also machines.

"Gideon"-Smirin
27   Israel 1991   W

"Gideon" is a software program running on ChessMachine hardware. It won the 1991 world championship for microcomputers, and here it encounters a strong grandmaster in an 'active chess' tournament.

Gideon's operator in this game reports:

"Smirin told me that he had never played a chess computer before, and he expected it to be interesting. In the earlier stages of the game he smiled a lot and made some jokes. At the end he said that he did not appreciate the amount of trouble the computer would cause him." [16]

1   ♗g4?!

The turning point of the game. Black expected his opponent to play weakly, and here it seems that White has obliged. This caused the grandmaster to relax . . .

1   ...   ♗b7?
2   e5!

With disastrous consequences for Black, who had to surrender a central pawn.

White won, despite tough resistance from his distinguished opponent.

4 Common Failures in the Sensing of Danger: Position-Related Factors

I. When the situation looks familiar

The opening phase in a battle between experienced chess professionals is usually played at a very fast rate. This is because the position on the board is well-known to the protagonists and play does not involve real thinking, since that part was done at home, before the game started.

Some middlegame schemes are also handled in a superficial manner, being part of a player's common knowledge, and hence not requiring special treatment.

Familiarity breeds a sense of safety, whilst unfamiliarity arouses a feeling of alertness.

However, it so happens that from time to time one encounters a position that one *wrongly* assumes to belong to the basket of the 'regular', 'well-known', or 'routine', while this, in fact, is not so.

Nothing special seems to be happening in the following diagram. We are just out of the opening stage, and the position resembles many others resulting from queen's pawn openings.

**28   Kozma-Korchnoi
Luhacovice 1969   W**

1 Rad1?

Still, one careless move is enough for a sleepy position to explode.

The text enables Black to carry out a winning combination based on the lack of flight squares for White's queen and bishop.

1 ...   c4!

| 2 | bxc4 | dxc4 |
| 3 | ♛xc4 | |

The alternative was 3 ♗xc4
♖c8 4 ♛b3 (or 4 ♛d3 ♗e4) 4 ... b5
5 ♗d3 (5 ♖c1 ♖xc4 6 ♖xc4 ♗d5)
5 ... ♗d5! and the queen is
embarrassed.

| 3 | ... | ♖c8 |
| 4 | ♛b3 | ♗d5 |

And in view of the inevitable 5
♛a4 b5 6 ♛xa6 ♖a8! 7 ♛xb5 ♖a5
White resigned. A beautiful domi-
nation of the queen.

Marangunić-Novak
29 Arbero (Student Ol.) 1966 **B**

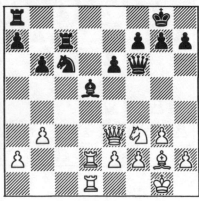

Black should feel quite comfor-
table in this very standard type of
position. His next move, however,
is a serious mistake:

| 1 | ... | ♖ac8? |

The shrewd combination that

follows is not easy to spot; but on
general considerations, he should
have made some air for his king
with 1 ... h6.

| 2 | ♘d4! | ♗xg2 |

1 ... ♘xd4? 2 ♛xd4 winning a
pawn due to the impossibility of 2
... ♗xg2? 3 ♛d8+.

| 3 | ♘b5!! | |

The sting. Black cannot play 3
... ♗d5 4 ♘xc7 ♖xc7 5 ♖xd5!.

| 3 | ... | ♖e7 |

Another clever point of White's
combination is revealed in the
variation 3 ... ♗h3 4 ♘xc7 ♖xc7 5
g4! ♗xg4 6 ♛g3 with a decisive
double attack.

| 4 | ♔xg2 | g6 |
| 5 | ♖c1! | |

White is in total control.

5	...	e5
6	♖dc2	♖e6
7	♘xa7	♘xa7
8	♖xc8+	♘xc8
9	♖xc8+	♔g7
10	a4	♖d6
11	♖e8	♖d5
12	♛f3	♛d6
13	♖e7!	♛xe7
14	♛xd5	♛c7
15	b4	

And **Black resigned** after a few
moves.

II. The sound of silence

Most chess players react swiftly to the signal of *noise*. When our king is surrounded by a host of hostile forces, we interpret this as an alarm signal. When the tactical complications are numerous, or the time factor is critical (as in a race between opposite passed pawns), the average chessplayer perceives this as a loud alarm: "Keep looking" or "Beware".

But what if the situation on the board fills us with a sensation of peace and quiet? Here we can draw valuable conclusions by way of analogy with the field of parenthood.

For a mother whose small children are *too* quiet, the sound of silence is a strong signal for alarm. The father, hearing no child-nagging for a complete hour, senses that something could be very wrong.

No news is bad news in this particular case. Sometimes, this is true in chess too.

(diagram 30)

What could go wrong for Black in a position like this? 1 ... ♖e4 looks simple and good. But so does Black's actual choice!

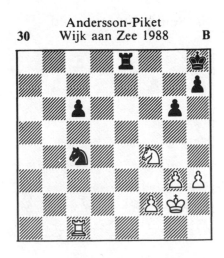

Andersson-Piket
30   Wijk aan Zee 1988   B

| 1 | ... | ♘e5?? |
| 2 | ♖e1! | |

Some dangers appear from a clear sky. Black cannot now avoid heavy material losses. He cannot get out of the pin, nor can he place his rook in a protected position (were his pawn on c7 instead of c6, he could have saved himself by 2 ... ♖e7 3 ♘d3 ♘c6).

2	...	♔g7
3	♘d3	♔f6
4	f4	♘xd3
5	♖xe8	c5
6	♔f3	Resigns

(diagram 31)

Black deliberately went in for the position in diagram 31, inviting White to win a pawn by 1 ♘xe5 ♘xe5 2 ♕xa5.

Stutzkovski-Harmonist
31 Berlin 1898 **W**

Question 4: White accepted the invitation, evidently seeing nothing wrong with it. What would you do?

Petrosian-Najdorf
32 Santa Monica 1966 **B**

In this boring position Black offered a draw. Petrosian writes:

"I declined, which my opponent

evidently did not expect, and he quickly replied with **1 ... 🨜d4?**.

If Najdorf had taken the trouble to ponder a moment, he would have noticed that White had slight chances to win. But being convinced that *any* move would result in a draw, he moved. 1 ... 🨝c3 would really draw." [17]

2	🨗xb5	🨝c3

2 ... 🨝b6 3 🨜a6.

3	🨜a8+	🨔g7
4	🨗e8!	🨜xb4
5	🨜a7	

So, White had won a pawn, and with his famous skill of converting small advantages into victory Petrosian won the game in another fifty moves. The lesson of this is that it almost never pays to act hastily, and that even a barren position can contain poison.

III. The dark side of being in a dominating position

In certain positions one tends to lose one's sense of danger because the enemy is, apparently, without good options.

The next diagram is a good illustration of this phenomenon.

1 🨔g2, defending against the mate, was reasonable, although Black of course can draw by 1 ... 🨛a2+.

33 Larsen-Keres
San Antonio 1972 **W**

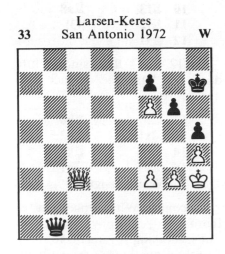

Larsen made what he thought to be a winning attempt:

1	g4	♛h1+
2	♔g3	♛g1+
3	♔f4?	♛h2+
4	♔g5?	♛g3!

Karpov, who was one of the competitors in this event, relates:

"(During analysis) we came across an amusing variation, in which Larsen could even lose, if he should carry on regardless . . . Imagine our astonishment when . . . (we) called in at the tournament hall . . . we saw Larsen's king had climbed voluntarily into the mating net."[18]

5 ♛e3

The position is worthy of careful study. White is tied up because he has to guard against ... ♛e5 mate.

5	...	hxg4
6	♛f4	♛xf3
7	♛xg4	♛e3+
8	♛f4	♛e2!

It transpires that White is losing f6 as well: 9 ♛d4? ♛h5+ or 9 ♛d6? ♛g2+ are disastrous.

9	♛g3	♛h5+
10	♔f4	♛f5+
11	♔e3	♛xf6

And **Black won**.

34 Petrosian-Korchnoi
Moscow 1963 **W**

In this dominating position White played the incomprehensible

1 ♖xh6?

Petrosian later explained[19] that he overlooked Black's answer, "possibly because it was in contrast to Black's hopeless position". 1 ♔f3 was correct, keeping the advantage.

1 ... f3!

2   ♔g5

2 ♔xf3 ♔g7+!.

2   ...   ♔e8!
White resigns

Kevitz-Capablanca
35   New York 1931   W

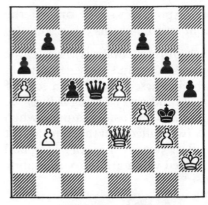

A pawn up, it is difficult to
believe that White faces any
danger of losing, but indifferent
play hands Black the initiative:

1	♖d1	g6
2	♔h2	a5!
3	♕e2	b5
4	f4	a4
5	bxa4	bxa4
6	♖d2	a3!
7	g4?	g5!
8	♕f2	

8 f5 ♕e5+ 9 ♔h1 ♖c1+ 10 ♖d1
♕b2 11 ♕e1 ♖xd1 12 ♕xd1 ♗xa2
is losing.

8	...	♕xf2
9	♖xf2	gxf4

10	♖f3	♖a8
11	♖f2	f3!
12	♗f1	

Or 12 ♗xf3 ♖b8, since White
does not have the defence ♖f3
any more.

12	...	♖b8
13	♖xf3	♖b2+
14	♔g3	♖xa2
15	♖c3	♖a1
	White resigns	

Of course, White's play was far
from good, and one could point
out several improvements for him.
But the main thing to remember is
that White lost because, as commentator Chernev put it,[20] "he
must have been blissfully ignorant
of danger".

Mikhailov-Beresovsky–Klovan
36   Riga 1974   W

The diagram describes a variation on what happened in the
actual battle. Black appears to be

dominating, but this impression is misleading. In fact, placing his majesty at g4 entangles Black in great trouble.

1 f5!   ♔xf5

Forced.

2 e6!!

A Greek gift. Capturing the pawn takes a square from the king, allowing 3 ♕f4 mate.

2	...	♕d8
3	exf7	♔f6
4	♕e8	♕d2+
5	♔h3	

And White wins.

37   Larsen-Spassky
Linares 1981   **W**

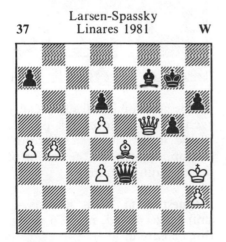

The white king is in check. Since 1 ♔g4?? h5 is helpmate, and 1 ♗f3, self-pinning, is just silly, there remained two logical possibilities: 1 ♕f3 and 1 ♔g2.

Question 5: What is your choice? Is there something wrong with these moves?

38   Belyavsky-Adams
Haifa 1989   **B**

Here is one of the least dangerous situations one can find oneself in: a rook ending a pawn up!

1	...	g5
2	♔g2	♔g7
3	♔f3	♔f6
4	♔e4	b5
5	♖c1	♖b8
6	♖c3	♔g6
7	h4	h6

"(Naturally) White should not lose . . . but should he win?! The end of the game is . . . tragicomic" – Sergei Makarichev.[21]

8	h5+!	♔xh5
9	♖xf7	bxc4?
10	♖f6!	cxb3?
11	g4+	♔xg4

12	♖g3+	♚h5
13	♖h3+	♚g4
14	♖fxh6	♖b4+
15	♔e5	Resigns

Since mate follows. Quite incredible, when you consider the diagram position, don't you think?

IV. When there are (almost) no pieces left

To sense danger, one has first to recognise an energy source that can create threats. The fewer forces our rival possesses, the less alert one tends to be to the possibility that some danger is lurking beneath the surface. But as long as our adversary is left with something, even a minimal and unimpressive army, a constant risk remains. After all, even a lone king can cause trouble, by way of stalemate.

Hutter-Wust
39 Vienna 1939 **W**

1	♖h8??	

A natural move, but allowing the black king access to the f-file proves deadly:

1	...	♔f1!
2	♖xh3	♘g4

With mate next move.

Dombrovska-Lisovska
40 USSR 1988 **W**

The position is a draw, because even if White loses his pawns, Black is left with a "wrong" bishop, opposite to the colour of the queening square h1.

Question 6: Well, if it is so simple, go ahead, make a draw! But be careful . . .

In diagram 41 White will have to give up his rook for the advanced black pawn, and the resulting ending will be a draw. However, it is

Rogers-Shirov
41 Groningen 1990 **B**

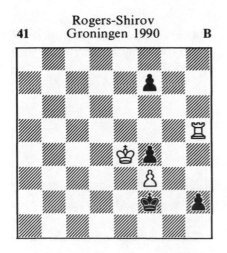

not *that* easy. The young star of the black pieces was of the opinion that all roads lead to Rome, and chose

1	...	♔g2??
2	♔xf4	h1=♕
3	♖xh1	♔xh1

– only to be embarrassed after

4 ♔g3!

Here **Black surrendered**, observing his hopeless situation after 4 ... ♔g1 5 f4 ♔f1 6 ♔f3 ♔e1 7 f5 ♔d2 8 ♔e4 ♔c3 9 ♔d5 ♔b4 10 f6.

Had he been alert to possible danger, he would surely have found another path, which does draw: 1 ... ♔g3! 2 ♖h8 f5+ 3 ♔xf5 ♔xf3 4 ♖xh2 ♔g3 =.

One wonders how it is possible for Black to lose in the next diagram. True, White has a better pawn structure and Black's pieces are tied to the defence of his pawns, but the scanty material makes the win virtually an impossible task.

Gutman-Nindl
42 Vienna 1986 **B**

Indeed, after a sensible continuation like 1 ... ♖b5 2 ♔g2 ♖a5 3 ♔f2 h5 the draw is clear.

Instead, the conclusion was

1	...	h5??
2	♖xe5+!	♖xe5
3	f4+	**Resigns**

3 ... ♔f5 4 fxe5 ♔xe5 5 ♔h4 ♔f6 6 ♔xh5 etc.

Notice that ♖xe5+ was not a threat in the diagram position, which means that one has to look for *potential* dangers, in addition to *actual* ones.

In diagram 43 a Black player

really has to be cooperative in order to lose!

Dr Krejčik-NN
43   Vienna 1939   **W**

1 ♖e6+   ♔h5??

Sometimes one makes a decision by a process of elimination; 1 ... ♔f5/f7 loses a pawn, and ... ♔g7/h7 appears passive; so let's try another move. The trouble is that that one's the worst!

2 ♖xe5+   Resigns

(diagram 44)

Not a particularly complicated position, one might think: 1 ♖c8 ♔g2 2 ♖g8+ ♔h3 3 ♖c8 apparently takes care of Black's two advanced pawns and draws.

Question 7: Check carefully the above variation. Spot the flaw, and find the right path for White.

Csanadi-Forintos
44   Budapest 1963   **W**

In the position in diagram 45, 1 ♖c5 ♖c8 (1 ... ♘g6 2 c8=♕ ♖xc8 3 ♖xc8 ♘xe7 4 ♖c7) 2 ♖b5! would put a swift end to the game, e.g. 2 ... ♘g6 3 e8=♕ ♖xe8 4 ♖b8.

Vaganian-Vasyukov
45   USSR Ch. 1974   **W**

Instead, White "discovered"

1 ♔e3??

which permitted a saving shot:

1 ... ♘d5+!

and the **draw** was inevitable (2 ♖xd5 ♖xe7+ with 3 ... ♖xc7).

Klaman-Gusev
46 USSR 1967 **W**

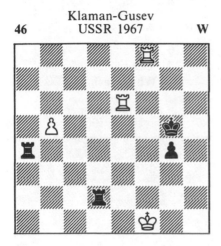

No position is so strong that it cannot be ruined by some bad play.

1	♖f2	♖d1+
2	♔g2?	♖aa1
3	♔g3	♖g1+
4	♖g2	♖a3+
5	♔h2	g3+!!

White resigns

A draw is the obvious result of the next diagram, but Botvinnik kept nagging at his adversary for many moves. White finally relaxed his vigilance for a moment, forgetting to pay his distinguished opponent due respect. Punishment came swiftly:

Suetin-Botvinnik
47 Moscow 1952 **W**

1	♖h4?	♖g3+
2	♔e4?!	♗d2
3	♗d3?	♗g5!
4	♖h5	

Otherwise 4 ... ♖g4+ winning a pawn and the game.

4 ... ♔c5!

Oh dear. Out of a quiet and uneventful ending Black has conjured a mating net! Since 5 ♔e5 ♖xd3 6 ♖xg5 ♖d5+ would lose, White preferred to admit failure at once. **White resigned.**

V. Moves that bring a false sense of security

Some moves bring with them a feeling of assurance. Castling can serve as a good example.

Generally beginners do not rush to castle in the early stages, and most chess manuals consider this as one major reason for their lack of success. Experienced players, on the other hand, tend, as an automatic habit, to castle as soon as possible. It is worth pointing out that sometimes the very move that intends to bring the king into safety is a grave mistake. In certain cases it is precisely the early notification of the king's address that enables the opponent to launch a strong attack.

Barczay-Udovčić
48　　Zagreb 1969　　**W**

1　0-0-0??

Very bad. In the present situation Black is bound to win the attacking race on opposite wings.

| 1 | ... | ♛a5 |
| 2 | ♚b1 | b5 |

3	♗d3	c4
4	♗e4	♖b8
5	♘d4	b4

The folly of White's first move is apparent.

6　♘xc6

Or 6 ♗xc6 bxc3.

| 6 | ... | dxc6 |
| 7 | cxb4 | ♗xb4 |

White resigns

Korotkov-Stupeni
49　　USSR 1965　　**W**

1　♗h5!　　0-0?

This provokes a vehement onslaught. Correct was 1 ... g6 and if 2 ♗e2 (2 ♘xc6 bxc6 3 ♛d4? e5) 2 ... f5 3 ♘c3 ♛e5.

2	♗xf7+!	♖xf7
3	♖xf7	♚xf7
4	♛h5+	♚g8

4 ... g6 loses to 5 ♛xh7+ ♚e8 6

♘f6+!.

| 5 | ♘g5! | ♗d6 |
| 6 | ♕xh7+ | Resigns |

| 50 | Liebert-Tabor
Hungary 1970 | B |

The black set-up does not suggest that he has any malice aforethought. Surprisingly, White's last two moves (0-0, h3) allow Black to develop a very strong initiative, even from his "innocent" structure.

1	...	♘g6
2	♗e3	h5!
3	♕d2	♗d7
4	b4	♕c8

This attack has chances of success *only* because White castled prematurely.

5 ♘g5?

5 h4!.

| 5 | ... | h4 |

6	g4	♘xg4!
7	hxg4	h3!
8	♘xh3?	

It cannot be said that White puts up strong resistance; but also after the comparatively better 8 ♗f3 ♗xg4 9 ♕d1 ♖h4! his game would not be enviable.

8	...	♗xg4
9	♘g5	♗xg5
10	♘e2	

Despair. If 10 ♗xg5 ♗f3! 11 ♕e3 then Black can choose between the simple 11 ... ♗xg2 12 ♔xg2 exd4, or the fancy 11 ... ♖h1+ 12 ♗xh1 ♕g4+ 13 ♔h2 ♕h5+ 14 ♔g3 ♘f4!.

10	...	♗f3
11	♘g3	♘h4
12	♗xg5	♘xg2
13	dxe5	♕h3
	White resigns	

Another move that makes us feel well protected is a checking move. "Always check, it might be mate" or "As long as I check I'm alive" are familiar aphorisms. Indeed, when a player makes a check, he rarely considers this as a dangerous move to *himself*.

With a two-pawn advantage White felt happy in diagram 51. He decided to insert a checking move, probably "just to see what's happening".

Tomović-Sokolov
51   Belgrade 1961   **W**

1   **Ee5+??**   **♔f2**

Suddenly a mate in two is threatened (2 ... Eh1+!) and White is defenceless. **White resigned**.

A massive exchange of forces is another situation which raises self-assurance that all is well. Below are two examples by ex-world champions, who initiated (Smyslov) or did not object to (Spassky) the emptying of the board by mass exchanges, only to realise subsequently that by this very step they had ruined their position.

Korchnoi-Spassky
USSR Championship 1956

1	d4	♘f6
2	♘f3	g6

3	g3	♗g7
4	♗g2	0-0
5	b3	d6
6	♗b2	e5
7	dxe5	♘g4
8	0-0	♘xe5
9	♘xe5	dxe5
10	♘c3	♘d7
11	♕d2	♘f6
12	♕xd8	Exd8
13	Efd1	Exd1+
14	Exd1	

The exchanges have not improved Black's position; quite the contrary.

52   **B**

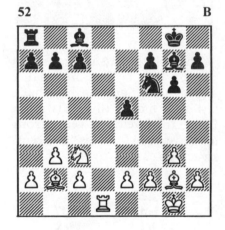

14	...	♗f5
15	♗xb7	Eb8
16	♗c6	♗xc2
17	Ec1	♗f5
18	♘b5	♗h6
19	Ec4	♗e6
20	Ea4	Ed8
21	♗xe5	Ed1+

22	♔g2	♖c1
23	♗f3	♘d5
24	♘d4	♗g7
25	♗xg7	♔xg7
26	♖xa7	♔f6
27	♘xe6	fxe6
28	♖a5	♘c3
29	a4	e5
30	♖c5	**Resigns**

Smyslov-Bronstein
Teesside 1975

1	d4	♘f6
2	♘f3	g6
3	c4	♗g7
4	♘c3	0-0
5	♗g5	d6
6	e3	c5
7	♗e2	♘c6
8	0-0	♗f5

53   **W**

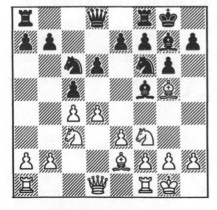

9   dxc5

White initiates a series of exchanges, desiring to end the game peacefully. This policy is wrong, since with every exchange Black improves his situation.

9	...	dxc5
10	♕xd8	♖fxd8
11	♖ad1	♘e4!
12	♘xe4	♗xe4
13	b3	h6
14	♗f4	♘b4!
15	a3	♘a2
16	♖xd8+	♖xd8
17	♖d1	♖xd1+
18	♗xd1	♘c3
19	♘d2	♗d3

And in view of 20 ♗f3 (20 ♗g4 f5 21 ♗f3 e5 22 ♗g3 e4, or 21 ♗h3 g5 and 22 ... g4) 20 ... e5 21 ♗g3 e4 22 ♗g4 f5 23 ♗h3 ♘e2+ 24 ♔h1 ♘xg3+ 25 hxg3 ♗c3 when the knight is lost, **White resigned**.

A move that captures one of the opponent's pieces (or pawns) also tends to foster our confidence in a misleading manner.

In the next example, White showed commendable restraint. In diagram 55, however, he didn't ...

(diagram 54)

1 ♗xb6 is very tempting: 1 ... axb6? 2 ♖xb6+ or 1 ... ♖g1+? 2 ♗xg1+ leads to a White victory. However, White noticed that Black had prepared a nasty answer.

Cordovil-Schumacher
54 Portugal 1970 **W**

Meduna-Varnusz
55 Hungary 1978 **W**

If **1 ♗xb6** then **1 ... ♔a8!!** is a winning reply: **2 ♖d1** (to prevent loss of the queen after 2 ... ♖g1+) **2 ... f3!!** and White can give up.

Having spotted this, White cleverly avoided the danger and played 1 axb6! ♖g1+ 2 ♖xg1 ♕xd3 3 bxa7+ ♔b7 4 ♖g7+ ♗c7 5 ♖xc7+ ♔xc7 6 a8=♕ ♕f1+ and the players agreed to split the point.

(diagram 55)

Black has sacrificed the exchange in return for a strong initiative. In the diagram position the correct move was 1 ♕c1, when the possible continuations 1 ... ♕h5 2 ♘xg4 ♘xg4 3 h3 or 1 ... ♖c8 2 ♕d2 ♖c2 3 ♕d3 would have left the result in doubt.

White decided on

1 ♘xg4?

based on the conviction that it is generally useful to capture or exchange one of the enemy's attacking pieces. While this is usually true, in the present situation it leads to a loss by force.

1	**...**	**♘xg4**
2	**♗f3**	**♘xh2!**
3	**♔xh2**	

3 ♖d1 ♖xd1+ 4 ♕xd1 ♘xf3 5 exf3 ♕xg3.

3	**...**	**♗f2!**
4	**♖g1**	**♖d6!**

White resigns

5 ♗h5 ♕xh5+ 6 ♔g2 ♕xe2 7 ♕f1 ♕e4+ 8 ♔xf2 ♖f6 mate.

5 Common Failures in the Sensing of Danger: Thought-Process-Related Factors

I. Real vs. imaginary dangers

In the process of looking for possible dangers, we are sometimes prone to the mistake of *false* identification; that is, envisaging a danger which does not exist, or worse still, missing the real threat, the actual source of trouble.

Hence the search for dangers should not stop at the point where one has (ostensibly) been found. It is essential to verify whether this is indeed the crucial danger, or if there are other, more severe threats that should be handled as top priority.

(diagram 56)

Black has taken measures to stop the advanced white g-pawn. Surprisingly, it is the modest a-pawn which carries the day:

56   Zimenau-Maier   **W**

| 1 | ♖f8! | ♖xf8 |

1 ... ♗xf8? 2 g8=♕.

2	gxf8=♕	♗xf8
3	a4	c5
4	a5	cxd4
5	cxd4	♗g7
6	♔d3!	Resigns

In the position in diagram 57, the advanced white passed pawn could be expected to play a

43

crucial role in deciding the outcome of the game. Since Black
has blockaded it, he appears to be
safe. But again, the danger springs
from another source.

Gulko-I.Gurevich
57   Philadelphia 1991   **W**

1	♕e8+	♚h7
2	♗d2!	♕c4
3	♗g5!!	

The continuation 3 ♘g5+ ♚g7
4 ♘xf7 ♕c2 5 ♗h6+ ♚h7 6 ♖c1
♖xd7 7 ♕xd7 ♕xc1+ 8 ♗xc1
♘xd7 would not be convincing.

3	...	♘xd7
4	♕e1!!	

So the d-pawn has gone, but
suddenly Black is tied up, the pin
along the d-file being very annoy-
ing.

4	...	♕a4

4 ... ♚g7 5 ♗xf6+ ♚xf6 6

♖xd7! or 4 ... ♗xg5 5 ♘xg5+ ♚g7
6 ♕e7.

5	♗xf6	♖e8

Black finds an ingenious defence,
but he cannot hold on for long.

6	♘g5+	♚h6
7	♘xf7+	♚h7
8	♘g5+	♚h6
9	♘f7+	♚h7
10	♕d2	♘xf6
11	♕h6+	♚g8
12	♕xg6+	♚f8
13	♖f1	♕c6
14	♘g5	♖e7
15	♖d1	♖g7
16	♕f5	

16 ♖d8+ ♚e7 17 ♖e8+ was
simpler.

16	...	♖e7
17	h4	♚g7
18	h5	**Resigns**

Nezhmetdinov-A.Zaitsev
58   USSR 1964   **B**

Black's position appears to be satisfactory. "Perhaps I should avoid any trouble in connection with 1 b4 followed by 2 ♗e4," mused Black, and he played

1 ... ♖d8?

It transpires that his fears were groundless. After 1 ... 0-0 2 b4 ♘b7 he is fine. Now, however, having delayed castling and abandoned control of the a-file, he really is in trouble!

2 ♘b3 ♖xd1+
3 ♕xd1 ♘b7

Black's discomfort begins to show. 3 ... 0-0 4 ♘xc5 ♕xc5 5 ♗e3 ♕c7 6 ♗b3 is clearly better for White.

4 a4 a6
5 axb5 axb5
6 ♘bd4!!

A lovely combination, leading to a ferocious attack on the black monarch.

6 ... exd4
7 ♘xd4 ♕d7
8 ♘xe6 ♕xe6
9 ♖a8+ ♘c8

9 ... ♔f7? 10 ♖xh8 ♗xh8 11 ♗b3.

10 ♗b3! ♕d7
11 ♕e2+ ♔d8
12 ♗e6 ♖e8

Everything is forced.

13 ♖xc8+! ♕xc8
14 ♕d1+ ♔e7
15 ♗xc8 ♖xc8
16 ♕e2+ Resigns

Lasker-Steinitz
59 World Championship 1894 W

Black is a piece ahead, and since his enemy's pride and joy, the advanced h-pawn, is firmly blockaded, he thought that he would soon collect the full point.

1 ♕h6! ♖e7?

Black could have attained a draw by 1 ... ♕e7 2 ♕f8 (2 ♖f8 ♖e6) 2 ... ♕xf8 3 ♖xf8 ♘g6 4 ♖g8 ♖h3. GM Ludek Pachman writes:

"Steinitz . . . was still dreaming about winning . . . He saw that 2 ♖f8 ♖xh7! was not possible for White but *he failed to see the main danger* [author's italics] – his exposed king." [22]

2 ♕h2! ♕d7

2 ... ♖e6 3 ♕f2+ ♔c6 4 ♖f8. Or
2 ... ♕d8 3 ♕g1+ ♔b5 4 a4+!
♔xa4 5 ♕c5! ♖e1+ 6 ♔a2 ♕xf6 7
b3+.

3	♕g1+	d4
4	♕g5+	♕d5
5	♖f5	♕xf5
6	♕xf5+	♔d6
7	♕f6+	**Resigns**

Dr Ehrlich-Shamai
60 Israeli Ch. (semi-final) 1984 **W**

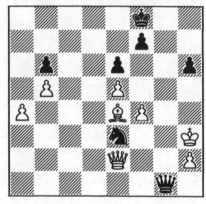

| 1 | a5 | ♘d1?! |

Black decides to ignore White's
play on the queenside, assuming
that his threats against the white
king will be stronger. In retrospect,
he should have played 1 ... bxa5 2
b6 ♘d5.

| 2 | ♕g2 |

2 a6? ♘f2+ 3 ♕xf2 ♕xf2 4 a7
♕e3+! wins.

| 2 | ... | ♘f2+ |

| 3 | ♔h4 | ♕e1 |

The crux of Black's plan. But
he was soon to be disillusioned.

4	a6!!	♘xe4+
5	♔h5	f5
6	♔g6	♕c1
7	♔h7!	♕c7+
8	♔h8	

Black can somehow handle the
a-pawn, but not the king! What
he imagined to be a weak piece in
his adversary's camp has been
transformed into a tower of
strength.

8	...	♘g5
9	♕a8+	♔e7
10	fxg5	hxg5
11	♔g8	

11 a7 was good enough.

11	...	♔d7
12	♔f7!	♕c8
13	♕xc8+	♔xc8
14	♔xe6	

The king alone has annihilated
Black.

14	...	f4
15	♔d6	f3
16	e6	**Resigns**

In diagram 61 White saw a danger in the variation 1 f7 ♕e5+!,
when 2 ♕xe5 or 2 ♕f5+ will be
defeated by 2 ... g6 mate.
Consequently, he chose

Sherbakov-Arlazarov
61 USSR 1972 **W**

1 fxg7?

But he had confused the real danger with the fictitious one. While his actual move was countered by **1 ... ♕f7+!** drawing by stalemate, his rejected 1 f7 would in fact clinch the win: 1 ... ♕e5+ 2 g5!! ♕xe6 3 f8=♘+!.

Romanovsky-Platz
62 St Petersburg 1916 **W**

White has identified the black e- and g-pawns as dangerous. Since in the diagram position they are safely blockaded, he allowed himself the move

1 a5

Question 8: Show the defect in White's concept.

II. Paying insufficient attention to the other side's plans

The importance of objectivity in a chessplayer's approach is stressed in many instruction manuals. It is imperative, so we are told, to assess the position as it is, without letting our desires and emotions interfere. We must neither become over-optimistic nor downright pessimistic.

Well, we certainly must try to do that. However, being only human, we *do* have some biases, and it is better to recognise them and try to improve, rather than pretend to be saints.

One of the most common biases is the tendency to concentrate on our own possibilities while underestimating the opponent's counterplay. According to Mark Dvoretsky, this trait is already shaped during childhood.[23]

Even the problemists and study composers, who are supposed to be free from emotional involvement and from preference for the 'White' or 'Black' sides of their creations, have difficulties in maintaining objectivity. They too are interested parties, just like competitive players. They want White to win (or draw, or mate in four, or whatever).

A player with a good sense of danger should put himself in his adversary's shoes, looking at things from his angle, insisting on finding good moves *for him* as well.

Yung-Rogman
63   1937   W

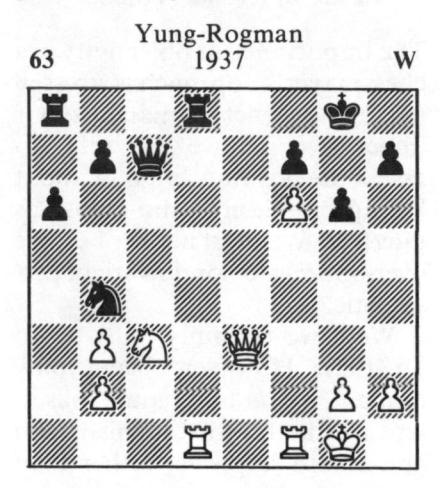

Here is a good demonstration of the not uncommon error of calculating a variation without seriously considering various possibilities for the enemy.

Black concluded that he should not fear 1 ♕h6 because of 1 ... ♕c5+ and 2 ... ♕f8. Notice that on the second move no White alternatives were analysed in this

reasoning. Black focuses on his own moves, neglecting to delve into the mind of his rival. In the present case, Black's error is exposed at once:

1 ♕h6   ♕c5+
2 ♖d4!!

Loss of a piece is unavoidable. **White wins**.

Anand-Timman
64   Tilburg 1991   B

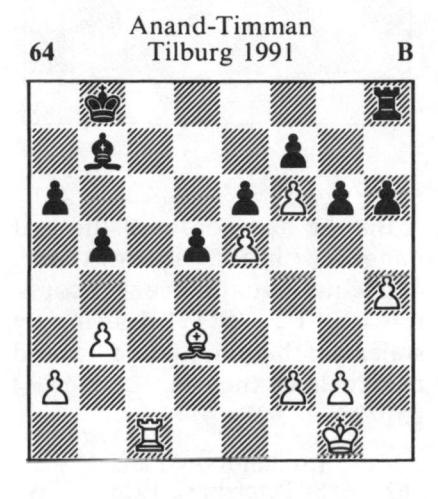

One does not have to be a grandmaster to realise the superiority of the White position. The pawn structure on the kingside guarantees that a bishop ending will be won for White (1 ... ♖c8? 2 ♖xc8+ ♔xc8 3 ♗xg6) and meanwhile White intends to create a passed pawn. Above all, what can Black do?

1 ...   g5
2 h5   ♖d8

3 f3

3 b4! d4 4 鲁c5.

3	...	d4
4	罝c5	奧d5
5	鲁f2	鲁b7
6	g4	鲁b6
7	罝c2	a5
8	鲁g3?	

White is oblivious to his enemy's plans. He sticks blindly to his own plan, and does not sense the approaching danger.

8	...	a4!
9	bxa4	奧c4!

Suddenly the black d-pawn reveals its power. If 10 奧xc4 bxc4 11 罝xc4 d3 12 罝c1 d2 13 罝d1 鲁c5 the white king is too far away. Of course, if he had only had the faintest suspicion that such a turn of events was possible, White would have kept his king in the centre . . .

10	奧e4	d3
11	罝d2	鲁c5
12	鲁f2	鲁d4
13	a5	b4
14	奧b7	罝d7
15	a6	奧d5
16	罝b2	鲁c3

White resigns

Diagram 65 is a quiet position, in which the issue revolves around whether the backward c6 pawn can be held. The lack of material makes it difficult for Black to organise an aggressive action against the white king.

Csom–Davidovic
65   Israel 1989   **B**

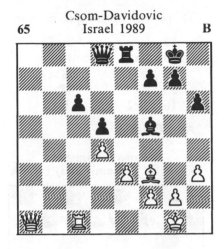

1	...	豐f6
2	豐a4	罝c6
3	豐d1	豐g5
4	鲁h2	豐h4
5	豐e2	罝f6
6	罝a1	g6
7	罝a2	h5
8	鲁g1	鲁g7
9	罝b2	豐g5
10	鲁f1	豐h4
11	罝b3?	

Black has made a lot of progress, while White has just waited, in the belief that he cannot be touched.

| 11 | ... | 奧g4! |

"Incredibly" – writes eyewitness IM Malcolm Pein – "all the spectators had seen this coming, but it came as a big surprise to the grandmaster." [24]

12 e4

There was nothing to be done.

12	...	♗xf3
13	♖xf3	♖xf3
14	♕xf3	♕xe4
15	♕c3	♕b1+
16	♔e2	h4

And **Black won**.

Tamari-Porath
66 Israeli Ch. (semi-final) 1971 **W**

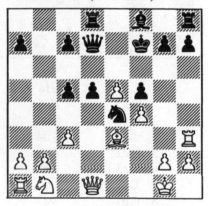

Black's whole set-up is directed towards creating a strong, advanced d-pawn. His previous moves, including ... c6-c5 and ... ♖a8-d8, lend support to this assumption.

1 ♘d2   d4?

Consistent, but wrong. Had he been more alert, trying to penetrate into his opponent's mind, he would have preferred the less

ambitious 1 ... ♘xd2.

2	♘xe4	fxe4
3	f5!!	

Completely changing the picture. Black is now subjected to a violent attack.

3	...	♕xf5
4	♕b3+	♔e8

4 ... ♕e6? 5 ♖f1+ ♔e7 6 ♗g5+.

| 5 | ♖f1 | ♕d7 |

5 ... ♕g6 6 ♖g3.

6	♖xh7!	♖xh7
7	♕g8	♕e7
8	♗g5!	

Crushing. After 8 ... ♖h8! 9 ♖xf8+! ♔d7 10 ♖xd8+ ♕xd8 11 ♕d5+ it is all over. In the game Black allowed a shortcut:

8	...	♕xg5?
9	♕f7	**mate**

Ruderfer-Dvoretsky
67   Odessa 1972   **B**

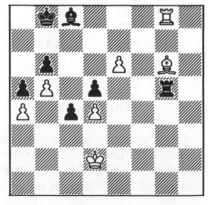

Black is completely lost, owing to the powerful white e-pawn. Observing the futility of 1 ... &c7 2 &xc8+ &xc8 3 e7, Black came up with one last trick before capitulating:

| 1 | ... | &b7!? |
| 2 | &xc8?? | |

Again, such a mistake stems from forgetting to ask oneself a simple question: "What is the enemy up to?".

| 2 | ... | &g2+! |

It was only now that White discovered that he cannot escape from the checks, since his king must not set foot on the e-file – e.g. 3 &e1? &xg6! 4 e7? &e6+. Hence, a **draw** was agreed.

68 Sax-And.Martin **W**
Hastings 1984

A healthy pawn up, White underestimates his adversary's

chances:

| 1 | &h5? |

1 &c5 was correct. White is too preoccupied with his own plan.

1	...	&c6!
2	&xh7+	&f8
3	&c5+	

3 &h8+ &e7 4 &g5+ &d7 5 &d4+ &c8 6 &d8+ &c7! wins.

| 3 | ... | &xc5 |
| 4 | &g1 | |

4 &h8+ &e7 5 &e4+ &d6! provides a nice echo of the previous note.

4	...	&e1
5	&h8+	&e7
6	&d4	&h3+

And **White resigned** because he is mated after 7 &h2 &h1+! 8 &xh1 &c6+.

69 Verduga-Soltis **W**
US Open 1983

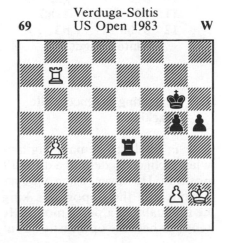

This position is a plain draw. However, some moves ago White had made a crude error, and now he is chasing the win that is no longer there!

1	b5	♖b4
2	♖b8?	♔f5
3	♔g3?	

Perhaps acting on the premise that his half point is guaranteed any time he so wishes; 3 b6 ♔g4 4 ♖a8 was an elementary draw.

3	...	h4+
4	♔f2	♔g4
5	b6?	♖b2+
6	♔f1	♔g3
7	b7	g4!

Not 7 ... ♖b1+ 8 ♔e2 ♔xg2 9 ♖g8! =.

8	♔e1	♖b1+
9	♔e2	♔xg2
10	♖g8	g3!
11	b8=♕	♖xb8
12	♖xb8	h3

White resigns

III. Neglecting defence while attacking

One is likely to remain vigilant when obliged to defend a difficult position. However, when a player is attacking the opponent's king he is usually in a party mood. He tends to become optimistic about his chances, and as a rule does not expect something vicious to happen to his own position.

Alapin-Marshall
70   Ostend 1905   **B**

1	...	♗f2+
2	♔d1	0-0
3	♗d2	♘xc3+
4	♗xc3	♕xd5+
5	♔c1	♖d8

We have not attached question marks to Black's moves, since what is wrong here is not a specific move but the whole concept: Black has been operating under the impression that he holds the initiative and that White is defending.

6   b4!

Renewing the threat of 7 ♕xf2, while preventing the defensive 6 ... ♗c5.

6	...	♗b6

7 ♕e7   Resigns

7 ... ♕d7 8 ♗c4+ ♔h8 9 ♗xg7 mate.

Boden-Bird
71   1897   B

With his queen and two bishops placed in threatening posts, White believed he was the aggressor.

**1   ...   f6
2   ♗xf6?   d5!**

Not 2 ... ♖xf6 3 ♕xc5.

**3   ♗xe7   ♕xe7
4   exd5   ♖xf2!!**

Suddenly it appears that Black has a crushing attack. If 5 ♕d1 (5 ♔xf2?? allows mate in one) 5 ... ♖xf1+ 6 ♔xf1 cxd5 followed by 7 ... ♕e3; or 5 ♖xf2 ♕e1+ 6 ♖f1 dxc3+. So **White resigned**. [Perhaps this was premature in view of 7 d4! ♕xf1+ 8 ♔xf1 ♗g4! 9 ♘xc3 ♖f8+ 10 ♔e1 when White emerges with a winning position – *Ed.*]

Euwe-Eliskases
72   Netherlands 1938   W

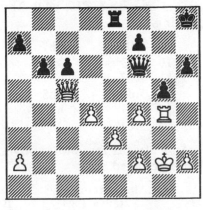

1	fxg5	♕e6!
2	♕e5+	♕xe5
3	dxe5	♖xe5
4	gxh6	♖a5
5	a4	b5
6	axb5	cxb5
7	♖g7?	

Commentator P.Schmidt remarks perceptively:

"The reason for this error must be psychological. Black has not been able to move by his own free-will since his 33rd move (the first after the diagram). Rather, his moves have been forced. And when one believes that an opponent can make only forced moves, one becomes careless." [25]

Correct was 7 ♖f4.

| 7 | ... | b4 |
| 8 | ♖xf7 | a6! |

Now, if 9 ☖b7 ☖b5 wins. Were White's rook on f4 he could counter 7 ... a6 with 8 ☖f6! b4 9 ☖b6, drawing.

9	☖f8+	♔h7
10	☖f7+	♔g8
11	☖d7	b3
12	☖d1	☖b5
13	♔f3	b2
14	☖b1	a5

And after a few more moves, **White resigned.**

Aloni-Matulović
73   Netanya 1961   B

| 1 | ... | ☖b8! |
| 2 | ♔a1 | ♘xg4? |

Black has an overwhelming attack, and by 2 ... ☖xb2! 3 ♔xb2 ♘d5! he would have achieved a beautiful victory; but thinking only about his own attack (3 fxg4? ♛xc3!), he now allowed his opponent a miraculous shot:

| 3 | ♗b6!! | ♛xb6 |

3 ... ☖xe2? 4 ♗xa5 ☖xc2 5 fxg4 ☖bxb2 6 ☖e8+.

| 4 | ♛xe8+ | ♗f8 |

Black is lucky to have this defence; 4 ... ☖xe8 5 ☖xe8+ ♗f8 6 fxg4 was winning for White.

5	♘a4	♛d8
6	♛xd8	☖xd8
7	♘d4	♘f2
8	♘xf5	

8 ♘c6 ☖xd6 probably gives Black sufficient counterplay.

| 8 | ... | ♘xd1 |
| 9 | ☖xd1 | |

9 ♘e7+ ♔g7 10 ☖xd1 ♗xe7.

9	...	gxf5
10	d7	f6
11	♘b6	♔f7
12	♘xc4	♔e6

And after some thirty more moves the players agreed to a **draw.**

(diagram 74)

White's pawn structure leaves much to be desired. Capturing on e4 with either the queen or rook was good enough for equality; but Black felt that he was dictating the course of the battle, and overestimated his chances:

Pietzsch-Cappello
74   Havana Ol. 1966   **B**

Grunfeld-Stepak
75   Israeli Ch. 1982   **W**

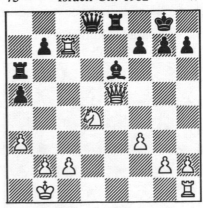

1	...	♕e5?!
2	0-0!	♖xb2
3	♕a4	

Perhaps Black only now saw that 3 ... ♕xg3 fails to 4 ♖xf7+!! ♔xf7 5 ♕d7+ winning.

| 3 | ... | ♕e7? |

Correct was 3 ... h4!, e.g. 4 ♕d7 ♖xg2! =.

| 4 | ♖a7 | ♖b7 |
| 5 | ♕a1! | |

A marvellous winning move. The double threat of 6 ♕xh8+ and 6 ♖a8+ is decisive. **Black resigned**.

(diagram 75)

White had every reason to feel happy. A pawn ahead with the better position, he seemed on his way to scoring his fourth consecutive victory in the tournament.

| 1 | ♕c5 | |

Simpler was 1 ♕f4 or 1 ♘xe6 ♖axe6 2 ♕c3.

1	...	♗d5
2	♘f5?	♖ae6
3	♕c3?	

White continues to operate under the impression that he holds the initiative. His moves are all very natural, but . . .

| 3 | ... | ♖e5! |

Incredibly, White is now losing a piece and the game! For instance, 4 g4 ♕xc7! is curtains.

4	♖d1	♖xf5
5	b3	h5
6	♖xb7	♕g5
7	♖b5	♗e6

And **Black won**.

It is not easy to spot the exact moment at which the initiative changed hands in the next position.

Manin-Ruderfer
76   Tashkent 1979   W

In the run-up to the diagram Black has played ... e4-e3 and ... f5-f4, restricting the mobility of the white bishop on g2. However, in order to achieve this he has had to open his king position, and he must now play very carefully.

1	gxf4	gxf4
2	♔h1	♗f6
3	♖g1	♔h8
4	♖ad1	♗d5?
5	♖d4!	♗e5
6	♕d3	♖d7
7	♗h3!	

The white bishop has freed itself with great effect.

7	...	♕xh3
8	♖xf4!	♗xf3+
9	exf3	Resigns

IV. When victory is in sight

Perhaps *the* most dangerous moment in a game is, paradoxically, just before victory is achieved.

When the game seems to be over, when everything is apparently decided and the resignation of our rival seems only a matter of time, many players ease up, drop their level of alertness, and expect the game to win itself.

But, as chess sages have repeatedly emphasised over the centuries, it is possible to ruin *every* position, no matter how strong it is.

"There is a temptation to relax when you are winning. Resist it!," advises IM Simon Webb, "Until he resigns, you have work to do." [26]

A version of the same theme occurs when the game reaches a "dead drawn" position, but our rival refuses to stop the clock and split the point.

"If you start asking yourself the question 'Why is he playing on?', be warned! This is always a dangerous state of affairs as it's easy to relax, lose concentration and let him play the 'sneaky' trick that he prepared while you were killing time." – GM Glenn Flear [27]

Mark Dvoretsky made the point with lucid simplicity: "There are neither absolutely drawn, nor absolutely hopeless positions." [28]

Csultis-Bade

77 East Germany 1972 **W**

1 ♕c7

Expecting – not without justification – Black's resignation.

| 1 | ... | ♖d1+! |
| 2 | ♖xd1 | ♖g2+! |

Some players become more
ingenious and more resourceful
when they are up against the wall.
But of course, if White does not
fall for 3 ♔xg2? ♕c2+ his victory
will be assured.

| 3 | ♔h1 | ♕c2 |
| 4 | ♕d6? | |

Holding a vast material advantage, White fails to sense any
danger. 4 ♖d2! would put an
immediate end to the game, and
4 ♖c1 ♕d3 5 ♕d6 is also quite
sufficient.[29]

| 4 | ... | h5 |

| 5 | ♗e5? | ♔h3 |

Suddenly White is mated . . .

| 6 | c6 | ♖xh2+ |

White resigns

Ivanov-Dolmatov

78 Novosibirsk 1976 **B**

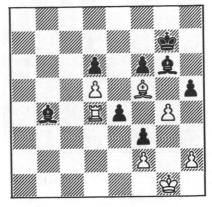

Why is Black continuing the
struggle?

| 1 | ... | e3! |
| 2 | ♖xb4? | |

Amazingly, this greedy collecting of further material gains
throws away the win. After 2 fxe3
Black would probably resign.

2	...	e2
3	♖e4	♗xf5
4	gxf5	h4!!

An incredible position. A rook
up, White cannot win. His king
is shut in the corner, and his rook
must stay guarding the e-pawn.
Draw!

When the position is *totally* won, one tends to become blasé.

Bakulin-Alexiev
79   USSR 1965   **B**

| 1 | ... | ♛d1? |
| 2 | ♗d2 | |

The first sign of trouble: the black knight cannot move on account of 3 ♗h6+. But Black is not yet perturbed . . .

| 2 | ... | b4? |

2 ... h5.

| 3 | h4! | |

With the threat of h4-h5-h6 mate!

3	...	♛c2?
4	♗h6+!	♚xh6
5	♛f8+	♚h5
6	♚h3!	g5
7	♛xf7+	♛g6
8	g4+	♚h6
9	♛f8+	♛g7

| 10 | hxg5+ | **Resigns** |

Miles-Short
80   London 1980   **B**

Three pawns down, White's resistance seems to be futile.

| 1 | ... | ♗a4? |

1 ... e3 intending 2 ... ♗e4 was crushing.

2	♛a3	♖c8
3	♘e3	♛a5
4	♖c1!	h5

Black now discovers that his intended 4 ... ♛xa7 5 ♗b5! ♖xc1+ 6 ♛xc1 will not secure the win, owing to the double threat 7 ♛c8+ and 7 ♛a3. "During my game against Miles, I was playing Space Invaders," recalls Short with embarrassment.[30]

5	♗d5!	♖xc1+
6	♛xc1	♛xa7
7	♛c8+	♚h7

8 ♘f5!   ♝e8

Searching for a win that has already slipped away. If 8 ... gxf5 9 ♕xf5+ draws by perpetual check.

9	♘xg7	♕d7
10	♕xe8	♕xd5
11	♘e6	♕b3+
12	♚c1	♕c3+
13	♚d1	♕f6
14	♘g5+!	♕xg5
15	♕f7+	♚h8
16	♕f8+	♚h7
	Draw	

Rogers-Korchnoi
81   Biel 1986   **B**

With his last move (1 c4!) White created enough counterplay to ensure the draw. 1 ... ♕e1 2 ♕b6+ gives a perpetual check, since 2 ... ♚e5?? 3 ♕c5+! ♚f6 4 ♕g5 is mate.

Korchnoi erroneously considered the position to be an elementary win for him, and although these moves were played shortly after an adjournment resumption he produced the appalling sequence

1	...	♕d4
2	♕d8+	♚c5??
3	♕c7	mate!

Heinicke-Rellstab
82   Oeynhausen 1939   **W**

Question 9: White has to be on guard in this winning position. Can you see what dangers await him?

(diagram 83)

White is two pawns up. His queenside pawns' road to glory is free. The knight's post at e5 is formidable . . . Everything seems very pleasant.

Now watch:

Iorkov-Chistyakov
83   Moscow 1961   **W**

1   ♘d3?   e5!

Obtaining some slight chances.
2 fxe5?? ♕f1 mate, or 2 ♖xe5?
♕xd3, or 2 ♘xe5 ♖c8 with an
initiative.

2   dxe5   ♖c8
3   ♕d4   ♖c2+
4   ♘f2??

Clearly he has not adjusted to
the changed situation.

4   ...   ♖xf2+!
5   ♔xf2   ♕c2+
6   ♔e1   ♕c1+
     White resigns

In diagram 84 Black is apparently continuing the fight in the
hope of a miracle. An experienced
White player should *actively search*
for the reason behind Black's
decision to battle on. He should

ask himself: "What traps might I
fall into? Where are his chances?
What possible errors on my part
might enable the enemy to find
salvation?"

Peli-Oratch
84   Israeli Ch. 1974   **W**

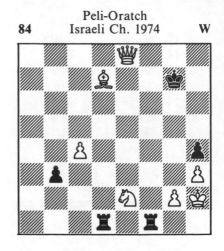

1   ♕e7+   ♖f7
2   ♕e5+   ♔h6
3   ♗f5   b2
4   ♘c3   ♖df1
5   ♗b1??

White walks right into it!

5   ...   ♖h1+!
Draw

6 ♔xh1 ♖f1+ 7 ♔h2 ♖h1+ 8
♔xh1 stalemate.

(diagram 85)

1 ... ♖ac8 is simple and strong,
after which Black would increase
his advantage. Instead, there came

Cnaan-Kaganovsky
85 Israel 1980 **B**

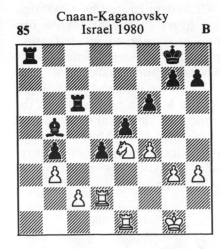

| 1 | ... | ♖a2? |

falling into the only trap available to his enemy!

| 2 | c4! | ♖xd2? |

After 2 ... bxc3! e.p. 3 ♖xa2 ♗d3 4 ♘f2 e4 he would still be in business; but demoralised after his former blunder, he errs again.

3	cxb5	♖cc2
4	♘xd2	♖xd2
5	b6	**Resigns**

(diagram 86)

Just as in the last example, the simple solution would do: 1 ... ♗xf6 followed by 2 ... ♕e5/d4 or 2 ... axb2. But Black wanted to get fancy, and chose

| 1 | ... | ♕e5? |

Segal-Shefi
86 Israeli Ch. (semi-final) 1965 **B**

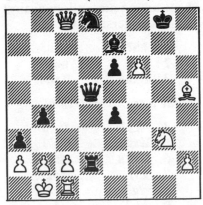

Question 10: It looks gloomy for White, but if you think for a while you will find enlightenment!

Torre-Maninang
87 Jakarta 1979 **W**

White has a big plus in the above diagram, as Black is cramped, with no serious counterplay.

This evaluation induced the White player to launch an attack without taking precautions against possible dangers:

1	h5?	gxh5
2	♕h4	h6!
3	♖xh6	♖xd4!

What a transformation!

4	♖g6?!	fxg6
5	♖xd4	♕e7!
6	♖xd8	♕xd8
7	♗f1	♕d2
8	♕g3	♕d4+
9	♔h2	h4
10	♕e1	♕f4+
11	♔h3	♗c6
12	♗e2	♕e3+
13	♔xh4	♗f3

White resigns

V. When the danger seems to be over

Imagine the following situation: your game has developed in an unsatisfactory way. You are under a lot of pressure. After great efforts you succeed in repulsing your opponent's waves of attack. The clouds seem to have lifted, you take a deep breath, and face the future with optimism . . .

Be careful! This could be a very awkward moment for you, since you are not prepared to meet any *new* dangers devised by your sly enemy . . .

Blunders caused by relaxation are likely to appear "When one has just emerged intact from a period of difficult defence", write Hartston and Wason.[31]

Likewise, the chess psychologist Victor Malkin observed that the opponent may take advantage "not only of negative emotional influences, but also of positive ones",[32] such as euphoria or relaxation.

Greenfeld-Rechlis
88   Israel 1988   B

A serious mistake at an early stage had left Black in deep water. Defending stubbornly, he achieved the position above, which is the best he could hope for under the circumstances. White's extra pawn is doubled and the black knight is placed on a strong, central post. After 1 ... ♖d6 Black would have chances of holding the position.

But believing that the main

dangers were behind him, Black relaxed and played

1	...	♖ac8?

This was countered powerfully with:

2	♗g4!	♖a8

2 ... ♖c7 3 b6 axb6 4 ♖xb6 is difficult for Black: 4 ... ♖d6? 5 ♖xd6 ♔xd6 6 ♖f6+ ♔c7 7 d6+; or 4 ... h5 5 ♖ff6!.

3	♗e6!!	♖f8
4	♗xf7!	♘xf7
5	e5	

Murderous.

5	...	♘xe5
6	d6+	♔d7
7	♖xf8	♖xf8
8	♖xf8	♔xd6
9	♖h8	h5
10	♖h7	b6
11	b3	Resigns

Kasparov-Psakhis
89 La Manga (match) 1990 **W**

Black had managed to get out of an unpleasant situation to reach the position above. GM Lev Psakhis relates:

"For the first time in the game I could utter a sigh of relief. Black has a reasonable organisation of his pieces, keeps a pawn advantage, and forces an exchange of queens. Moreover, White was left with only 15 minutes to reach the time control . . . Kasparov was of the opinion that his initiative was enough only for equality, *but he felt that Black sighed in relief too early* [author's italics] and decided to press on." [33]

1	♕xc7	♖xc7
2	♖fe1!	♖e7?!

2 ... h6!.

3	♘b5!	♖fe8
4	♖xe7	♘xe7
5	♗h3!	♗c8

Here and on the next move it was better to occupy c8 with the knight.

6	♗xc8	♖xc8?
7	♘xa7	♖c2
8	b4	♔f8
9	♗e3	♘f5
10	♗xb6	

And a few moves later **Black resigned**.

Diagram 90 shows the adjourned position after 40 moves. On his

36th move Polugayevsky had missed a winning line, and now Black had real chances to draw.

Polugayevsky-K.Grigorian
90   USSR Ch. 1973   **W**

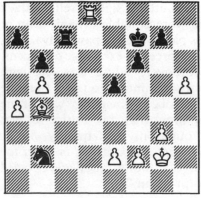

1 &d6   Rb7?

The first move after resumption and already a mistake! 'Polu' was severely critical of his adversary:

"He had no suspicion of the dangers threatening him . . . He should still be on his guard; why, in fact, does White part with his a-pawn and keep his bishop on the a3-f8 diagonal? Perhaps he has some aim . . . In short, there was plenty for Black to think about . . ." [34]

The game continued

2	e4!	&xa4
3	f4	

Black finds himself in a mating net. After 3 ... &c5 4 f5 &d7 he is totally paralysed.

3	...	exf4
4	gxf4	g5
5	e5!	gxf4
6	h6	&e6
7	Re8+	&f5

Or 7 ... &d5 8 &e7.

8	e6	**Resigns**

6 Combining Various Signals: The Concept of Discrepancy

So far we have been dealing with specific danger signals, from one source or another. However, in real life we sometimes encounter many fragments of data from several sources which are not always consistent.

For instance, we may be playing what we believe to be a very quiet and uneventful game. Strangely, the opponent looks very pleased and satisfied. There are no butterflies in our stomach, but people are beginning to crowd around the table, staring and whispering.

How should conflicting signals like these be interpreted?

Before trying to answer that, let me quote from Dutch chessplayer and psychologist A.D. De Groot. Considering the question "When does a chessplayer look for an improvement to his intended move?", he reached the conclusion that it is when the result of his analysis is at variance with the player's expected outcome – "The *discrepancy* being a *signal* that something is probably amiss." [35]

De Groot further observed that "Omissions and errors in calculation tend to remain undiscovered especially in situations where a discrepancy is lacking."

Relating the notion of discrepancy to our topic leads us to formulate a simple rule: when pieces of data (chessic or psychological) are supplied from several sources, *any discrepancy* between them should be regarded as an indication of a *potential danger*.

If we are winning, the opponent is supposed to look unhappy. When the enemy is in grave danger, we expect him to become anxious. If our position is strong, we should have a good feeling. If there is nothing interesting in the position, spectators are likely to move away to other boards.

If that is not so, something may be "fishy" and a danger signal should appear in our mind's eye.

Descriptions of such discrepancies are not widespread in chess literature, but that does not mean that the phenomenon is

65

unfamiliar. In a game against Hort in 1970, Petrosian chose a different move from the one he had intended, because "[he] was surprised to see a look of confidence on Hort's face".[36]

In another reported instance, Fischer refrained from playing a strong move against Tal (in 1959) because when he wrote it down before actually playing it, Tal made a gesture that Fischer misinterpreted as a laugh![37]

Miles-Peters
91   Lone Pine 1976   **B**

While waiting for his opponent's reply White had analysed some variations connected with the moves 1 ... ♖h7 and 1 ... ♖f8.

1   ...   ♖h7

According to Miles's previous calculations, this was supposed to lose in a straightforward manner to 2 ♖d8+ ♖xd8 3 ♕xd8+ ♔g7 4 ♕f6+ ♔g8 5 ♖e8+ ♘f8 6 ♖xf8+ ♔xf8 7 ♕d8+ ♔g7 8 ♗f6+ ♔h6 9 ♕f8+ ♔g6 10 ♕g8+! mating.

"I quickly wrote down his move . . . and then spent a few minutes wondering why he had played the 'easy' line" – Miles.[38]

The fact that his adversary had voluntarily entered a losing line switched on White's alarm signal. It didn't take him long to spot that 2 ♖d8+ ♖xd8 3 ♕xd8+ ♘f8! 4 ♖e8 (4 ♗e7 ♖g7+) fails to 4 ... f5+ 5 ♔h3 ♕xf3+!! 6 gxf3 ♗f1 mate!

Realising the danger, White played 2 ♗h6! ♘f8 3 ♖de7 ♗g6 4 ♔g5! and won the battle.

Since authentic material on the issue of discrepancy between signals is scarce, I shall draw on my own humble experience for the next two examples:

Grunfeld-Avni
92   Israeli Ch. 1984   **B**

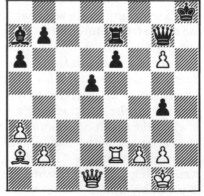

Black is better, and the move 1 ... g3 suggests itself. Indeed, I was about to play this, when I suddenly sensed that grandmaster Grunfeld's body had become tense, and that his arm was positioned as if he was ready to answer my move at once.

Since my evaluation of the position was not consistent with the signals I received from my opponent, I decided to have another look at the position. Soon I found the variation 1 ... g3? 2 ♖xe6!! gxf2+ (2 ... ♕h6 3 g7+!) 3 ♔f1 ♖xe6 4 ♕h5+ ♔g8 5 ♗xd5 (or 5 ♕xd5) which, if anything, is in White's favour. By playing 1 ... ♕xg6 Black side-stepped the pitfall and kept his advantage (though the game ended in a draw).

Avni-Gutkin
93   Israeli Team Ch. 1990   B

White is a pawn up but his pieces lack harmony. Black reacts

vigorously, before White can consolidate:

1	...	♕b8!
2	♕d3	♗f5
3	♕c4	♗e6!

I was quite surprised by this. Surely 4 ♕xb4 (not 4 d5? ♗xd5) 4 ... a6 5 ♘d6 ♕xb4 6 ♗xb4 ♗xd4 7 ♗a3 was advantageous for White, wasn't it? But my opponent had stayed very cool. Somehow, this behaviour didn't seem to fit together with his allegedly precarious position!

So a careful examination was called for; and then the truth appeared:

4 ♕xb4?   a5!!

And White is losing material: 5 ♕a4 ♗d7 or 5 ♖xa5 ♖xa5 6 ♕xa5 ♗c4 when both 7 ♘d6 ♗xf1 8 ♔xf1 ♕xb2 and 7 ♖c1 ♗xb5 are better for Black.

The game continued 4 ♕d3 ♗f5 5 ♕e2 and after many vicissitudes it ended in a draw.

In order to compare various danger signals, one has in the first place, to acquire the ability to perceive these signals.

I believe that chessplayers should open their eyes and ears to absorb signals from *outside* the chessboard. Of course, forming a strategic plan is important; calculating tactical variations is important;

but there is additional data that can be derived from other sources and that might be very handy in making decisions.

To illustrate the point, here is a vivid description by D.Schweitzer, a leading Israeli football coach, which I think is applicable to chess as well.

"A professional person can see, in the players' eyes, before the game starts, if they are facing defeat or victory. In the dressing-room, before the game starts, if every player is mustering his concentration and there is a healthy tension in the room, then all is well . . . But if they are chatting about every possible subject except the game, that attitude is bound to continue . . . and a loss is on its way . . .

I once saw [a certain team] entering the stadium. I noticed that the players were not calm . . . they were impatient, they could hardly wait for the referee to signal the beginning of the contest . . . I knew that they were going to tear the other team apart, which they did . . ." [39]

Danger signals can be detected in the opponent's appearance, his body language, his gestures . . . We just have to tune ourselves to perceive these signals.

However, drawing conclusions from off-the-board signals should not be taken to extremes. It is not the *only* source of data that should be considered:

94   Rabinovich-Romanovsky
Moscow 1925   **W**

1 ♗g5!

Obviously Black is in a bad way, facing the double threat of 2 e5 and 2 ♖xd3.

To understand what happens next, one has to take into account the following information:[40]

1) Romanovsky (the player of the black pieces) played the game in a state of illness that showed in his appearance.

2) He was very late for the start of the game, and was forced to move quickly in order to manage the time control.

These two factors probably led Rabinovich to believe that the game had already been decided. However, he forgot to pay attention to one vital piece of data:

3) There is still plenty of play in the position. Romanovsky at that time was a very strong player indeed, and dangerous even in such a desperate state of affairs.

Ignoring this last consideration proved costly:

1	...	♖fd8
2	e5?	

Later analysis proved the superiority of White's position after the correct 2 ♘e5!.

2	...	♗a3!
3	exf6	♕c5
4	♗d2	

Defending against the threat of 4 ... ♕xc3+ and intending to win by 5 ♕g5.

4	...	♗g6!
5	♕a4	

5 g4? ♕b4.

5	...	b5!
6	♕xa3?	

Or 6 ♕xb5? ♖ab8!! 7 ♕xc5 ♗xb2 mate. The lesser evil was 6 ♕b3, although after 6 ... b4 Black retains winning chances, e.g. 7 bxa3 ♖db8!.

6	...	♕f5!

With a two-piece advantage White cannot prevent mate! 7 ♕b3 ♖ac8 and there is nothing White can do about 8 ... ♕b1 mate.

White resigns

7 Developing a Sense of Danger

Now that we have discussed some of the various forms in which danger signals may appear, and are familiar with the difficult task of detecting them in good time, we can move on to the central question: how should one go about developing this skill of identifying dangers and recognising critical moments?

The author does not regard the sense of danger as some gift that one either has or does not have. Like other skills in chess, the art of sensing danger in time can be acquired and developed by training.

Here are some useful ways:

I. Shaping the right attitude

A) Adopting a paranoid approach

In chess, it is very useful to adopt what I shall call a "paranoid approach".

Seeing the world as a dark, unfriendly place where one is fighting for survival; being distrustful and cynical; always trying to find out where the "catch" is; assuming that enemies are haunting us; all these are usually regarded as negative qualities in real life.

They are, however, splendid qualities to possess as far as chess is concerned.

In a widely quoted article, Lord Taylor writes:

"There is only one place where, as a temporary expedient, a paranoid approach is a positive advantage – on the chessboard."[41]

Hartston and Wason, too, refer to the difference between behaviour on the chessboard and outside it, when they say:

"The chessplayer might well be advised never to trust his opponent, but we should be loath to offer such advice, for fear of possibly detrimental transference effects in real life."[42]

While the question of drawing the line is important (more than a few chessplayers are known to confuse chess with real life – Fischer and Kamsky are prominent followers of a "The world is

70

against us" attitude), it is undeniable that being distrustful and suspicious has clear benefits, chesswise.

GM Valery Salov, from the former USSR, opined:

"Probably this Soviet habit of always looking for enemies, this persecution mania, is not so bad when you are playing chess . . . Maybe this was one of the special features that helped the Soviets to play better chess." [43]

An empirical study, conducted by the author and others,[44] revealed similar findings. A group of strong and experienced chess players differed significantly on the paranoia scale of the MMPI psychological test from both weaker players and non-players. They emerged as more suspicious persons, with greater mistrust and more guardedness.

96   W

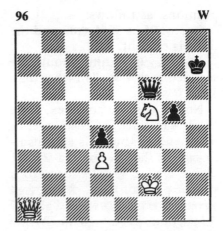

97   W

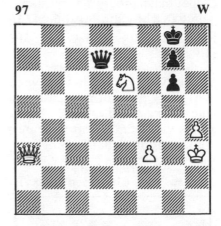

To exercise the paranoid approach, take a look at the three positions above, and then read the explanatory text that follows.

The three diagrams are very much alike. In all of them White enjoys an advantage of a knight, but that piece is pinned and its loss is unavoidable. Therefore, Black can achieve a draw in these

95   W

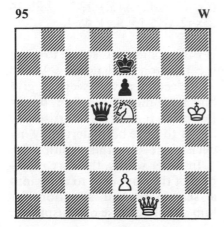

positions, as follows:

In No. 95, 1 ♕f4 ♚d6 and the draw is evident.

In No. 96 White should be satisfied with 1 ♕xd4 rather than 1 ♕a5? ♚g6.

No. 97 is more complex, since White can enter an advantageous pawn ending, but it is still insufficient for the full point: 1 ♕b3 (1 ♕f8+ ♚h7 2 ♕xg7+ leads to a similar position) 1 ... ♚f7 2 ♚g4 ♕xe6+ 3 ♕xe6+ ♚xe6 4 ♚g5 ♚f7 5 f4 ♚f8 6 ♚xg6 ♚g8 and White cannot make progress, for instance 7 h5 ♚f8 8 h6 gxh6 9 ♚xh6 ♚f7 10 ♚g5 ♚g7 and Black has the opposition.

Question 11: You don't have to trust every piece of nonsense you read! Take another look at diagrams 95-97 and form your *own* opinion about what's going on.

Wharton-Kotliar
98 New York Ch. (Open) 1988 **B**

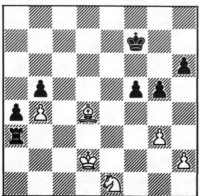

Black's rook is in a precarious position: 1 ... ♖b3 2 ♗c3, or 1 ... ♖a2+ 2 ♘c2 followed by ♚c1-b1 are in White's favour.

1	...	f4
2	♗c3	♖a2+
3	♘c2	fxg3
4	hxg3	h5!

Annotating the game, the Black player remarked: "My opponent should have wondered why I did not rescue my rook." Instead, naively believing that everything was fine, he played

5	♚c1?	h4
6	gxh4	gxh4
7	♚b1?	h3
8	♗e5	♖xc2!
9	♚xc2	♚e6
10	♗b8	♚f5
11	♚d3	♚g4

And **White resigned**, anticipating the variation 12 ♚e2 a3 13 ♗e5 (or 13 ♚f2 ♚f5!) 13 ... h2! 14 ♗xh2 ♚f5 15 ♗g1 ♚e4.

Both contestants strove to reach the position in diagram 99. The white centre pawns seem to give him a promising position, but as Petrosian remarked, "Portisch ... ought to have been alerted by my decision to play this position."[45]

In other words, the very readiness of the opponent to enter into a seemingly bad situation for him should arouse our suspicion.

Something along the lines of "It's too good to be true".

Portisch-Petrosian
99   Lone Pine 1978   **B**

| | 1 | ... | ♞c5! |
| | 2 | ♞c4? | |

An error, but he was in a bad way already: 2 dxc5? ♗xc5+ and 3 ... ♖xd2; or 2 d5 ♖ee8 with the threats 3 ... ♞d3 or 3 ... ♗f4; or 2 e5? ♗xe5; or 2 ♖e2 ♞a4 3 ♞c4 ♞xb2 4 ♞xb2 ♗f8.

2	...	♞xe4
3	♖ac1	♗f8!
4	♞e5	♞d6
5	a4	f6
6	♞f3	♖xe1+
7	♞xe1	♖d7
8	♞f3	♞f5

And in due course Black succeeded in converting his advantage into victory.

Hodgson-Norwood
100   British Ch. 1991   **B**

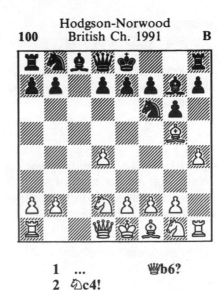

1	...	♛b6?
2	♞c4!	

Black should now have realised that his plan was refuted, and return his queen to d8. Instead, he interpreted White's last as an error and continued

3	...	♛b4+?
4	♗d2!	

Now Black is in deep trouble. Amazingly, he still thought that the blunders that have been made were on White's part:

"He played what I thought to be a horrific blunder . . . I could not believe this – giving me a piece for nothing . . ." – Norwood.[46]

3	...	♛xc4

3 ... ♛b5 4 e4 0-0 5 a4 is unpleasant, so this third consecutive

oversight may be the best.

4 ♜c1   ♕xc1

It was only now that the truth dawned upon Black: moving the queen allows mate.

5 ♝xc1   ♞c6
6 ♞f3

And in this winning position White agreed to a **draw**, which was sufficient for him to become his country's champion.

B) Maintaining a self-critical attitude

Not only has one to be suspicious of one's opponent, one must also remain sceptical of one's own conceptions.

A healthy dose of doubt, and double-checking of major decisions, can help to prevent awkward surprises.

GM Nikolai Krogius writes:

"I advise you to discipline yourself during the game, by mentally posing the question – 'Have I appraised the position/play/idea too hastily? Did I stop examining this variation too soon?'"[47]

(diagram 101)

1 ...   ♜fe8?

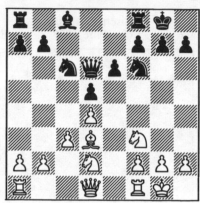

101   Tunik-Gubyanov
USSR 1976   **B**

Black's position is cramped, so his intention to gain some freedom through the advance ... e6-e5 is understandable. In retrospect, however, it was better to play this move right away.

2 ♜e1!   e5??

He should have double-checked his plans, and asked himself what the idea might be behind White's last move.

3	dxe5	♞xe5
4	♜xe5!	♜xe5
5	♞c4!	dxc4
6	♝xh7+	♚xh7
7	♕xd6	**Resigns**

C) Actively searching for possible dangers

Dangers can be found by accident,

or brought to light in a methodical searching process. It is the second way that we recommend. An active search for danger signals enhances the probability that a danger will be spotted (if one does exist).

Relating to a nasty pin a player found himself in, GM Andrew Soltis wrote:

"This kind of surprise pin can only be anticipated by a good sense of danger. 'Where are the potential pins?' 'If I'm pinned . . . how easy is it to get out of it?' These are the questions to ask yourself."[48]

Mortensen-Karlsson
Esbjerg 1989
102 W

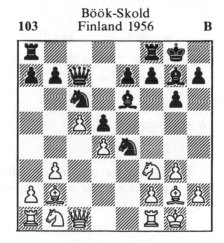

| 1 | ♖dh1 | h6 |
| 2 | ♖h3? | |

A natural continuation of the attack. 2 ♖g3 is on its way, while Black seems to be short of counter-

play . . .

| 2 | ... | ♖xf3! |
| 3 | ♖xf3 | ♘b4!! |

Astounding. After 4 axb4 ♗a4 we realise that the double sacrifice has cleared the way for the queen and bishop to attack c2. Wherever the white king tries to escape, he will be mated.

White resigns

The search for dangers is an *ongoing process*. Even when one source of danger has been recognised, the search must continue.

The following diagram is a case in point.

Böök-Skold
Finland 1956
103 B

Black's threats change constantly in the ensuing play. At every turn White has to face a new danger. In such a situation it is easy to miss something.

1	...	♗g4!
2	♘bd2	

d4 was hanging, and 2 ♕e3 was no good on account of 2 ... ♘xc5!.

2	...	♗h6
3	♕e1	

Defending against the threat to win a piece by 3 ... ♗xf3; but the removal of the queen from the queenside enables Black to stir up more trouble.

3	...	♘xd2
4	♘xd2	♘b4

Things are looking gloomy, but White finds a defence (at least he thinks he does!).

5	♘f3!	♘c2
6	♕e5	♕d7!!

6 ... ♕xe5? 7 ♘xe5 ♗e2 8 ♗xd5 would give White a lot of compensation. The text move creates yet another new threat, which White overlooks.

7	♖ad1	

He should have given up the exchange, since Black's reply gains something even more valuable.

7	...	♘e3!!

White resigns

8 ... f6 is not to be denied.

D) Thinking for the other guy as well

Finally, as was repeatedly mentioned in previous chapters, it is most helpful to look at things from the opponent's point of view. "Prophylactic thinking" is the term used by Dvoretsky.[49] It is this factor that differentiates the really strong players from the average ones.

Translated from words into action, it is clear that one ought to invest a considerable amount of one's allotted time in trying to fathom what is in the enemy's mind.

104　　Karolyi-Gelfand
Amsterdam 1988　　**W**

1	c6

Black has several obvious advantages in this diagram: better king position, better pawn structure and queenside majority.

Still, alertness is always required. White's first move contains a cunning threat which Black misses:

| 1 | ... | a4? |
| 2 | ♗e6!! | |

All of a sudden a white queen is going to appear on the board! Luckily for Black his position is so strong that he is able to hold the draw comfortably.

| 2 | ... | ♖xd2 |
| 3 | c7 | ♖f2+ |

Simpler was 3 ... ♖d3+ with a perpetual.

4	♔xf2	♘xe4+
5	♔e3	♘d6
	Draw	

Lautier-Hebden
105   French League 1990   B

| 1 | ... | a6 |

Would you interpret this move as the beginning of an attack on the white king? I bet you wouldn't!

| 2 | bxa6 | ♖xa6 |
| 3 | ♗xb7 | ♖xa5 |

So the situation on the queenside has clarified, which is what 1 ... a6 was all about. But look at the a5 rook: it has more freedom than it did three moves ago. One has to watch out!

| 4 | e3? | ♗xb7 |
| 5 | ♖xb7 | |

5 exd4? exd4.

| 5 | ... | ♕c8! |
| 6 | ♕b1 | e4!! |

Suddenly the plan of ... ♖h5 and ... ♕h3 becomes very powerful: 7 exd4? ♖h5 wins, or 7 ♔g2 ♖h5 8 ♖h1 ♖xh1 9 ♔xh1 ♕h3+ 10 ♔g1 ♘f3+ and Black collects a piece.

| 7 | ♘d5 | ♕h3 |
| 8 | exd4 | |

All the tactics work in Black's favour: 8 ♕d1 ♖a1!!.

| 8 | ... | ♗xd4 |
| 9 | ♖b8 | |

A beautiful variation could have occurred after 9 ♘xe4 ♖xe4 10 dxe4 ♕xg3+ 11 ♔h1 ♕h3+ 12 ♔g1 ♖a3! 13 ♘e3 ♗e5!.

9	...	♕xg3+
10	♔h1	♕h3+
11	♔g1	♕g4+
12	♔h1	♖a8
13	♖xa8	♖xa8
14	♕d1	♕h3+
15	♔g1	♗e5
	White resigns	

All this advice concerning the player's mental attitude originates from the basic precept of *treating the enemy with respect*. Easier said than done.

To take an analogy from military combat, here is what Brig. General R.W.Williams from the US army says:

"Assume, and honestly try to believe, that your opponent *is as smart as you* ... As a corollary to this rule, recognise that your opponent, being at least as smart as you, *always has a plan*. Not only does he have one, *he intends to win*. His objectives might be incomprehensible to us, but they are very real to him ... Somehow, we must eliminate the popular concept ... that the enemy is little more than a temporary impediment located between us and our objective."[50]

It is not easy to accept all this. As a matter of fact, it must be admitted that the aforementioned view is not always valid. It does happen that the opponent is *not* very clever, not playing with a certain plan in mind, etc.

However, having respect towards one's adversary is an essential prerequisite to forming a developed sense of danger. Indeed, if the enemy is assessed as worthless, what's the use of guarding against his plots?

II. Coaching techniques

When teaching others, it is essential to instil in them the apprehension that even in a seemingly secure or promising position a shocking and unpleasant danger *could* be lurking under the surface.

A) Demonstrating that every position is capable of being ruined

Kasparov-Tukmakov
106   USSR 1982   **W**

Black's plan to push his two extra pawns all the way is simple, crushing and unavoidable. It is difficult to think of any conceivable measure of counterplay that White can implement ...

| 1 | h4 | b4 |
| 2 | h5 | ♗xe4 |

Unnecessary, but it does no harm.

3	fxe4	b3
4	♖ad1	♖c7
5	♗g5	b2
6	♗h6	♕e7
7	♗g5	♕f8
8	♗h6	♕e7

Repeating moves, probably to avoid – or to get out of – time trouble.

9	♗g5	♕c5
10	hxg6	fxg6
11	♖d8!	

Of course, this should not bear fruit, but the fact that one can find some chances even in a hopeless position like this is instructive.

11	...	♖xd8
12	♗xd8	

Now 12 ... ♘e3 or 12 ... ♖d7 are decisive. In his defence, one has to say that Black's choice also looks good enough ...

12	...	♖b7??
13	♕f6!	♘xe5
14	♗c7!!	

But it's not!

14	...	♖xc7
15	♕d8+	♔g7
16	♕f6+	Draw

In positions like diagram 107, commentators usually make a dry remark to the effect that "Black could have spared us the rest by

resigning". Indeed, 1 ♕d8+ ♔g7 2 ♖c1 ♗d7 3 ♖c7 is one convincing reason for Black to give up.

Filip-Darga
107   Bled 1961   W

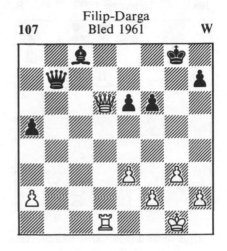

1	♕d8+	♔g7
2	h4?	♕f3!
3	♖c1	♗b7

Black has certainly improved his position a great deal, but White is still winning, of course.

4	♖c7+	♔g6
5	♕g8+	♔f5
6	♕xh7+??	

6 g4+ ♔e5 7 ♖c5+ still wins by force: 7 ... ♔d6 8 ♕f8+ ♔d7 9 ♕f7+ ♔d8 10 ♕c7+ ♔e8 11 ♕b8+ ♔f7 12 ♖c7+ with 13 ♕xb7.

6	...	♔g4!

It transpires that after 7 ♖xb7 ♔h3! White is mated ... **White**

resigned, probably shaking his head in disbelief.

van Wely-Wahls
108   Taastrup 1992   B

In a rotten position, Black tries to confuse the issue:

1	...	g4
2	♗e5	♛c8
3	gxf4	b5

Intending to put pressure along the a8-h1 diagonal.

| 4 | cxb6 e.p. | axb6 |
| 5 | f5 | |

From now on, White chooses second-best moves, allowing his cunning opponent to create counterchances. 5 fxg4 or 5 ♖d7 would have been safer and clearer.

| 5 | ... | ♖e7! |
| 6 | ♗b5 | |

6 ♗e2!.

| 6 | ... | gxf3+ |

| 7 | ♖xf3 | ♛a8 |

Things are getting more and more complicated.

| 8 | ♗xf6 | ♗xf6 |
| 9 | ♛xe3 | ♖g8+ |

Suddenly it is difficult to find a safe haven for the king.

| 10 | ♔h1 | ♖eg7! |
| 11 | a4?? | |

The crowning piece of carelessness, probably due to time shortage. 11 ♗e2 would have left the result in doubt.

11	...	♗d4!
12	f6	♛xf3+
White resigns		

B) Showing the effect of minor details on the overall outcome

Grasping the significance of small details in the appraisal of the overall situation helps us to develop the cognitive faculty that tells us when and where a danger is likely to emerge.

One possible coaching method is to show students a set of positions that are very similar in appearance but which conceal important differences.

Take a look at diagrams 109 to 112. What do you think of the White position (note that it is Black's turn to move)?

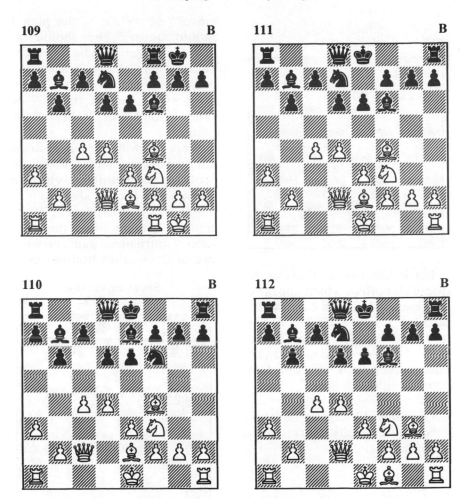

109 B
111 B
110 B
112 B

Question 12: The four diagrams look very much alike. White's position appears safe and solid in all of them. But if one looks closely enough, it transpires that in one of the diagrams this is not the case.

Perneder-Post
113   Berlin 1932   **B**

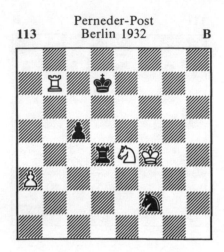

Black has two options at his disposal, both of which appear to be winning: **1 ...** ♔c8 2 ♖e7 ♔d8 3 ♖e5 (or 3 ♖e6 ♔d7) 3 ... ♘d3+; or **1 ...** ♔c6 2 ♖e7 ♘xe4 3 ♖xe4 ♔d5! 4 ♖xd4+ ♔xd4, and in the ensuing race Black will come first, promoting with check.

Question 13: Examine these variations carefully. Pay attention to minute details.

C) Using the "worst case" technique

Another way to improve the quality of young players' "danger-detectors" is to encourage them to look at their games from a somewhat different angle. In addition to asking oneself the usual questions like "What is the best move?" or "What is the plan I should choose?", they should implement "the worst-case technique", by posing themselves questions such as "How could my position become ruined?" or "How could I lose?" [GM Andrew Soltis[51]].

Were the following position a fairy chess problem, it would probably be entitled "White to play and lose in the shortest way possible". As it happened, White actually accomplished this in a serious tournament game between two of the world's best players.

Short-Belyavsky
114   Linares 1992   **W**

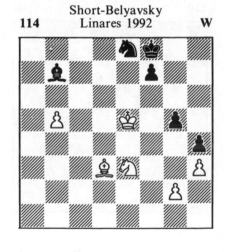

1	♘d5	f6+
2	♔e6??	♗c8
		mate (!!)

Naturally, GM Nigel Short was mated because he did not suspect anything remotely like a mating possibility could occur in such a simplified position. Similar accidents do take place from time to time, and if we are looking for prevention methods, rather than being content with the comforting sympathy of others, then searching for a possible catastrophe is as reliable a method as any.

Take the following diagram as an example. It is Black to move, and it looks very safe and equal for him (and boring). Try to examine all sorts of possible moves, with the intention of finding some vicious traps, a cunning pitfall or concealed threats.

**115   Wachtel-Musiol
                   Poland 1953   B**

Question 14: To make it simple, skip over the "obvious" bad moves, like 1 ... ♖e5?? and concentrate on "normal" responses like 1 ... b5, 1 ... ♖c4, 1 ... ♖c3+, 1 ... a6, 1 ... ♗g2, or 1 ... ♔a6.

Did you find anything?

*D) Maintaining a dynamic
   evaluation of the
   ever-changing situation*

Another technique that can be used is to demonstrate to students games characterised by many tactical twists. Says John Littlewood:

"It is important for our students to witness as early as possible the influence of tactics in the opening stages, so as not to be lulled into a false sense of security when apparently following the basic principles of opening play."[52]

Looking at the following short game, one could get the impression after nine moves that it is heading towards a peaceful conclusion. However, some inaccurate play by Black enables White to launch a brilliant sacrificial attack at lightning speed.

Godena-De Eccher
Italian Championship 1987

1	e4	c5
2	c3	d5
3	exd5	♕xd5
4	d4	♘c6
5	♘f3	e5
6	♘xe5	♘xe5

7	dxe5	♛xe5+
8	♕e2	

116   B

Only eight moves have been played, and the queens are already going to be exchanged. The position will probably soon better resemble an ending than an opening . . .

8	...	♝d6?
9	♘a3	♛xe2+
10	♝xe2	a6?
11	♘c4	♝c7
12	♝e3	b6
13	b4!	b5
14	♝f3	♜b8
15	♝xc5!	bxc4
16	♝c6+	♝d7
17	0-0-0!!	

Hard to imagine, but true! From a "boring" position, White has developed (with the help of his opponent . . .) a fascinating sacrificial attack within only a

117   B

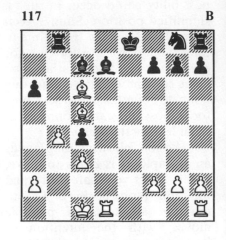

few moves! The picture after 17 ... ♝xc6 18 ♜he1+ is lovely.

17	...	♘f6
18	♜he1+	♚d8
19	♜e7	♝d6
20	♜xf7	♝xc5
21	♝xd7	♝f8
22	♝b5+	Resigns

Such a turn of events is not infrequent, and the sooner one recognises that, the sooner one will learn how to accustom oneself to changing circumstances.

The position in diagram 118 looks innocuous. No real confrontation between the two armies has yet occurred. Black is slightly better because of the backward white pawn at e3 and the potential "hole" at e4. White should continue 1 ♘f3 and if 1 ... ♘f5 then 2 ♜e1, and he is holding his own.

van Scheltinga-Pirc
118   Dubrovnik Ol. 1950   **W**

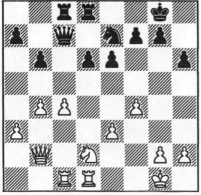

1	e4?	d5!
2	exd5?	♕xf4
3	dxe6	♕e3+
4	♔h1	♕e2!!

A tremendous move. The whole picture of the battle has changed dramatically: White is completely tied up and Black is in total command.

5	exf7+	♔f8
6	♕c2	♖d4

Even stronger was 6 ... ♖d3!.

| 7 | ♕h7 | ♖cxc4! |

Not 7 ... ♖xd2 8 ♖xd2 ♕xd2 9 ♖f1.

| 8 | ♖f1 | ♖f4! |

White's burst of initiative has come to a halt. Now there is no salvation.

9	♘f3	♖xc1
10	♖xc1	♖xf3

White resigns

E) Implementing a search for danger as a regular procedure

Still another valuable and proven method is to teach the need to be alert and suspiciously-minded as an integral part of the thinking process.

Dividing the thought process in a given position into specified and structured stages, Lev Alburt and Larry Parr categorise the last stage under the heading "Remain alert, snuff out counterplay".[53]

"In chess," the authors stress, "there is often one last mountain to climb." The opponent's moves will be easier to find if only we look for them.

Sanguinetti-Liberzon
119   Biel izt 1976   **W**

It is difficult to imagine that this position will be decided abruptly, in only one move, but that is what actually happened. By trying to fathom Black's intentions White could have avoided disaster, but his next move shows that he totally missed the fact that Black had a serious threat.

1   &f3??   d5!
White resigns

Since the loss of a piece cannot be averted.

Fostering a paranoid way of thought can be done by emphasising "rules of thumb" such as:

● Not every move that looks good is in fact so.

● Try to find out what is concealed behind the opponent's apparently innocuous moves.

● If the enemy deviates from his usual approach (such as his regular opening systems, or a familiar set of habits), be careful.

F) Studying double-edged positions

Working with players who focus too much on their own plans, while underrating the adversary's intentions, Mark Dvoretsky uses as learning material studies that contain resourceful play by Black,

thus forcing the solver to think hard for "the other side".[54]

A.Herbstman
Axaglazdra Komynisti 1954
120   1st prize   **W**

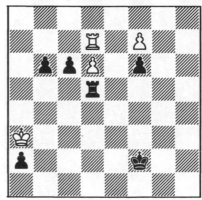

White wins

The diagram seems to be an easy win for White after **1 &xa2**. Strangely, **1 ... f5!!** forces a draw, in a fantastic way: **2 f8=&   Ia5+** with perpetual check along the a- to d-*files*. Alternatively, **2 Ia7 Ie5!!** and there is no way to prevent a perpetual along the fifth to the first *rank*.

Only by looking at things from the other side's point of view can a remarkable and well-hidden saving idea like this be exposed.

The solution is

1	&b2!!	a1=&+
2	&xa1	Ia5+
3	&b2	Ib5+
4	&c3	Ic5+
5	&d4	f5

6	♖a7	♖d5+
7	♔c3	♖c5+
8	♔b2	♖b5+
9	♔a1!	♖e5
10	♖a2+!	**White wins**

It was White's first move that made his tenth(!) possible.

1	...	e4
2	♘e6	e3
3	♘c5!!	e2+
4	♔d2	♘f1+
5	♔c1!	♔xe1
6	♘d3	**mate!**

from M.Liburkin
64 1935
121 joint 2nd prize **B**

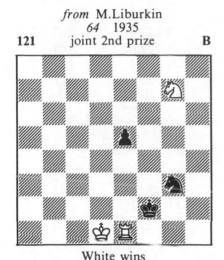

White wins

from
Kazantsev, Liburkin & Staroverov
Shakhmaty v SSSR 1933
122 5th H.M. **W**

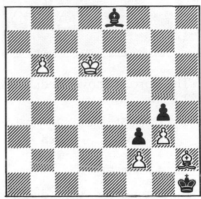

White wins

This diagram resembles the previous one, in that the situation looks virtually resignable for Black. The sequence 1 ... e4 2 ♘e6 e3 3 ♘d4 seems to put an end to Black's faint hopes. But ... wait a minute! Taking the variation a little further we suddenly realise that after 3 ... e2+! 4 ♘xe2 ♘f1! Black is saved: 5 ♘ moves ♘e3+ 6 ♔d2 ♘f1 (c4)+ draws. Only now, after the danger has been identified, is it possible to find a way to thwart it:

The advance 1 b7 queens the pawn. Black can do nothing about it, but astonishingly, he can still get a draw if White is not alert: **1 b7? ♗b5! 2 b8=♕ ♗f1!** and despite White's huge material advantage there is no win!

(diagram 123)

3 ♕b1 ♔xh2 4 ♕xf1 is stalemate, and other White fourth moves will be countered by 4 ... ♗h3, followed by 5 ... ♔g2 with an impregnable position.

123   **W**

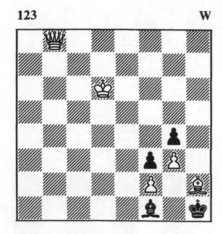

The correct move in diagram 122 is, therefore

1	♔c5!	♗g6
2	♔d4!	♗e8
3	b7	♗b5
4	b8=♖!!	

In comparison with diagram

123 White has achieved two important things: he has brought his own king closer to the black king, and has avoided the stalemate trap.

4	...	♗f1
5	♖b1	♔g2
6	♔e3	♗c4
7	♖b4	♗e6
8	♖b6	♗d7
9	♖h6!	♗c8
10	♖h4	♗d7
11	♔f4	♔xf2
12	♖xg4	

This was the aim of the previous moves. White liquidates into a winning pawn ending.

12	...	♗xg4
13	♔xg4	♔g2
14	♗g1!	

And wins.

8   The Art of Deception

"There is probably no aspect of warning so unpredictable, but so potentially difficult and damaging, as the efforts of the opponent to conceal his intentions . . . The deceiver may attempt either to lead his enemy to a totally erroneous decision, or to confuse him, by presenting him with a number of alternatives, thus promoting indecision" – C.M.Grabo.[55]

These are not the words of a chessplayer, but they could have been. Understanding the importance of danger signals inevitably leads us to search for means that will mask or conceal our plans from the opponent, and thus deceive him about our real intentions.

A cunning player may "plant" misleading clues in his play and/or in his overt behaviour, attempting to manipulate his enemy's conceptions, with the aim of leading him astray.

There is a thin line between carrying out a clever misguiding operation and behaving in an unethical way.

Chess players and psychologists Elliot Hearst and Michael Wierzbicki describe, under the headline of "Tricks and Gamesmanship":

[masters that] "developed the habit of thinking for 15 or 20 minutes on a move they had planned long before, [to] deceive their opponent as to the surprise value of his last move and perhaps lull him into a false sense of security."[56]

Other players, according to these authors, when realising that they have committed a blunder "get up and walk around happily" or "sit still and smile serenely".

On the other hand, IM Simon Webb regards such behavioural ploys as perfectly legitimate, and he actually encourages them:[57]

"If you are on the defensive, try to look completely dejected and uninterested, in the hope your opponent will get careless . . . When you set a trap, try to look normal, or even to appear nervous."

Trying to draw the line between the legitimate and the unethical, GM and psychologist Nikolai Krogius wrote:

"Camouflage is an acceptable method of struggle in chess. By 'camouflage' we mean trying to hide one's own feelings, not putting on deceptive scenes to upset one's opponent . . .[58]

Techniques for allaying the opponent's sense of danger

A) Masking

Luring the enemy into the heavy fog of ambiguity is not an easy task. The relevant chess data is all there in front of his eyes: how can one hide the obvious?

By way of disguise, the player makes a move or some moves that are not in accordance with his plan. He does not rush straight to his target, but rather approaches it indirectly. Metaphorically, it can be said that by the use of masking one walks sideways, backwards, maybe in circles . . . rather than straight ahead. Thus one makes it difficult for the enemy to predict the exact part of the board where things are going to happen, or the exact time when actions will take place, or the form they are going to assume.

Boleslavsky-Goldenov
124   USSR Ch. 1952   **W**

1 ♔c2!

White has been conducting a long manoeuvring battle, but the text move, as Shereshevsky correctly indicates,[59] is a camouflage for his true plan of action.

1	...	♖c7
2	♗b5	♖a7
3	♖d2	♔e7
4	♖e2	♔d6
5	♖e4	♘b6
6	♗f1!	♘d5?
7	♗h3	♘c7
8	♗g4	♖a8
9	♔c1!	

From the diagram position, had White played directly to attack the a4 pawn, Black could have defended successfully. But now, after confusing his enemy with seemingly aimless moves, White returns to the basic plan, at the most inconvenient moment for Black.

There is no doubt that placing the white king on c2, where it reduces the effectiveness of such a plan, contributed to the fall off in Black's alertness to danger.

9	...	♖a7
10	♗d1	♘b5
11	♗xa4	♘d4
12	♗d1	♘f5
13	♗g4	

And **White won.**

Konstantinopolsky-Ragozin
125 USSR Ch. 1940 **B**

1	...	♖fe7
2	h4	♕c7
3	h5	♖a7
4	♕d3	

White seems to have all the play, with the black king's defences about to crumble. Black's moves appear almost irrelevant.

4	...	♕d8
5	hxg6?	hxg6
6	♖xg6	

6 ♖h2+ ♖h7 7 ♖xg6 ♖xh2+ 8 ♔xh2 ♕h4+ 9 ♔g2 ♖h7 is no better.

| 6 | ... | ♖g7! |

It transpires that Black's heavy pieces, which have apparently been acting as defensive forces, are also able to assume a major *offensive* role! If 7 ♖xg7 ♕h4+ 8 ♔g2 ♖xg7+ 9 ♔f1 ♕h3+ winning. Another possibility is 7 ♖h6+ ♖h7 8 ♖gg6 ♖ag7!! and White is powerless: Black threatens 9 ... ♖xg6 and if 9 ♔g1 then ♖xh6! is a beautiful echo. 9 ♖xh7+ ♖xh7+ 10 ♔g2 ♕h4 is also losing.

All in all, an amazing "ambush". White played to open lines, but when that occurred he was doomed! The way Black had organised his heavy forces was one of the reasons for White's nonchalance.

7	♖6g5	♘e4
8	♖h5+	♖h7
	White resigns	

Hiding one's inner feelings

Observing their opponent's faces and body language is an important "intelligence-gathering" technique for chessplayers.

An outside spectator, even one ignorant of the finer points of the royal game, can usually recognise which side has the superior position simply by watching the expressions and the conduct of the contestants.

The best players take care to mask their behaviour. We must remember that a player mostly does not *know* how well things are going, he only *assumes*. The opponent's reaction can confirm or disprove this assumption, so it is therefore vital not to show the behavioural signs of defeat; rather, we should even try to confuse the antagonist as to our real feelings.

Former world champion Boris Spassky was reputed to have a "poker face". Looking at him, it was impossible to say whether he was winning or about to be mated.[60]

The motto seems to be "Do not give your opponent voluntarily *any* information".

For instance, learning to sit still after making a blunder, not giving one's feelings away, is an important skill for a chess player. "While awaiting his opponent's move, he remained absolutely calm. Not a muscle twitched on his face . . ." is how Roshal describes Karpov's behaviour during an embarrassing moment in a game against Gligorić.[61]

"Yet once he had seen [his blunder] . . .. with self-confident expression, just as if nothing had happened, he sat up before the table, showing his readiness to make his next move instantaneously" is a picture of Kasparov (vs. Kupreichik) drawn by Alexander Nikitin.[62]

Kagan-Partos
126   Biel 1977   **W**

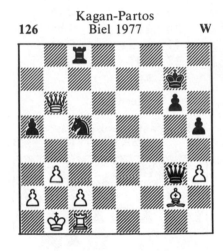

1	♗b7	♞xb7
2	♖g1!	♛d6
3	♖xg6+??	

3 ♛xb7+ leaves White with an advantageous ending. The text is a horrible oversight, intending 3 ... ♛xg6 4 ♛xb7+ and ♛xc8, but missing the refutation 3 ... ♔xg6!.

IM Kagan related the incident as follows:

"Realising the disaster at once, I sat at the board motionless. My rival, with twenty minutes for three moves to reach the time control, contemplated the position for three minutes, finally playing **3 ... ♛xg6??** and resigning two moves later."[63]

Disguising his feelings was White's only chance. Otherwise, Black would certainly feel that something was amiss. And this is in fact the usual behaviour of strong players. For example, in the game Weinstein-Rohde, Lone Pine 1977, White liquidated into what he thought to be a winning pawn ending, only to find out that the endgame was lost. According to annotator Kaplan:

"Even after noticing (his error), Weinstein kept a poker face and played his moves with great (apparent!) confidence. This is probably what saved the day for him!"[64]

B) Misleading

Here, the idea is taken one stage further. Not only is the opponent kept in ignorance about our real intentions, he is actually led to believe that something *else* is going on.

Ex-world champion Mikhail Botvinnik was pre-eminent in this respect. In one famous incident, he advised his compatriot Efim Geller in a complicated adjourned game against Fridrik Olafsson: "Rock about on your chair several

times, as many players do in a vain attempt to find a plan."[65]

In another instance, competing against Tal for the world championship, he side-stepped his usual habit of bringing a coffee thermos to the second session, and put about a rumour as well that he himself regarded his position as desperate. All this was intended to fill his adversary with a false sense of confidence, as Botvinnik himself revealed later.[66]

He thus raised the art of misleading the opponent to new heights, although the ethics involved are debatable.

127   Fuchs-Bronstein
Berlin 1968   B

1 ...   🜚fe8!

The greatest merit of this move is that one can easily miss the idea behind it, as White did, mistakenly believing it to be an overprotection of the e7 pawn.

2	♗e3?	g5!
3	♘h5?	

Still ignorant of what is to come. Naturally 3 ♘h3? g4 is futile, but 3 ♗d2 ♘c2 4 ♖c1 would have cut White's losses.

3	...	g4!
4	♘xf6+	exf6!
5	♕f4	♘d5

Only now did it dawn on White that the real purpose of 1 ... ♖fe8! was to weave a devious trap for White's queen. Alas, by now it was too late to do anything about it. **Black won.**

Nimzowitsch-Leonhardt
128   San Sebastián 1911   **W**

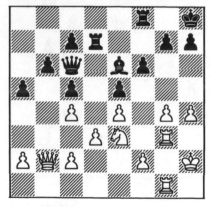

1	♖1g2	♕d6
2	♕c1	

How would you comprehend White's last two moves? Probably he wants to triple his heavy pieces on the g-file, to reinforce the advance g4-g5; or maybe he aims to initiate an attack through g4-g5 followed by ♕c1-d1-h5?

2	...	♕d4??
3	♘d5!	

Nothing of the sort! It was all a plot to invite the black queen to settle at the central post d4, where it will now be captured!

White wins, since no satisfactory reply against 4 c3 is available.

Spassky-Gligorić
129   Baden 1980   **W**

White's two bishops give him an edge, but Black's position is quite solid and hard to break down.

1	♕h5!	♖df8
2	♖f2	♔b8
3	♖af1	♘cd8
4	♔h2	b6?!

5	a3	a5?

White has built up some pressure on the kingside, and Black has been led to believe that it is there that things will be decided. But it is Black's carelessness on the other wing which will prove costly.

6	c3	♛d6
7	♛d1!	♖e8
8	b4	axb4
9	axb4	cxb4
10	cxb4	♞d4

Or 10 ... ♛xb4 10 ♛a1!.

11	♖a2	♛c6
12	♗xd4	exd4
13	♛a1	

Now it is clear that moving the pawns in front of his king was a grave error on Black's part.

13	...	♖e7
14	♖a7!	♛c2+
15	♔h1	♛xd3
16	♖c1	

Black could perhaps have spared himself the remainder.

16	...	♞c6
17	♖a8+	♔b7
18	♖xh8	♞b8
19	♗c8	mate

(diagram 130)

| 1 | ♖db1! | |

Hübner-Hort
130   West Germany 1979   W

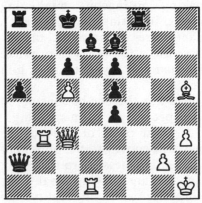

By protecting his rook on b3 White appears to threaten 2 ♛xe5 (which he does). But the "simple" threat is not the only danger Black is facing; identifying one danger does not necessarily indicate that *this* is the main one to guard against.

| 1 | ... | ♗d8? |

1 ... ♖f2 was correct, and if 2 ♛xe5 ♖f1+!.

| 2 | ♛c4! | |

New dangers emerge out of the blue: 3 ♖b8+, winning the queen, and 3 ♛a6+!, mating. Black cannot handle both threats at the same time. **White won**.

C) Provoking

Adopting a policy of marking

(chess) time and waiting for the other side to become active, making outrageous weakening moves, imitating the opponent's manoeuvres (symmetrical play) – these are a few ways to provoke the enemy, of trying to make him "let loose".

In a way this can be considered as a special type of misguiding.

A good piece of provocative play will convey to the opponent a deceptive message to the effect that we are playing weakly or aimlessly, while in reality the situation is quite different. When provocative play succeeds and the rival is driven to throw all caution to the winds, the provoker can reap his reward.

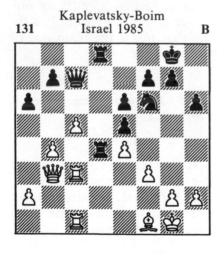

| | Kaplevatsky-Boim | |
| 131 | Israel 1985 | B |

1	...	♞d7
2	♔h1	♞b8
3	h3	♞c6

| 4 | a3 | ♛d7 |
| 5 | ♔h2 | |

An interesting moment. Black has a slight but clear superiority. He controls the d-file and has secured an excellent central post for his knight. But now, instead of carrying on with his plan (5 ... ♜d2, 6 ... ♞d4), he makes a move which gives an impression of hesitancy.

By this he induces White to take some action to prevent Black from occupying the excellent outpost at d4 with his knight.

5	...	♛e7!
6	b5?	axb5
7	♗xb5	♜d2!
8	♗xc6	

Black has willingly given his opponent the opportunity to exchange his bishop for Black's magnificent knight. White has been tempted only to be floored by the following combination, made possible because of the white bishop's sortie.

8	...	♜xg2+!!
9	♔xg2	♜d2+
10	♔h1	♛h4
11	f4	♛f2
	White resigns	

The next game began with White giving his rival odds of queen's rook and queen's knight.

Barnes-Amateur (odds game)
132   New York 1873   **W**

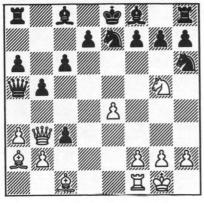

1 Ëe1!

What is this?! But remember that White is playing against a weak opponent. If he plays straightforwardly 1 Ëd1 Black might become suspicious . . . so, let's lead him to believe that White was in fact executing a gross blunder, and provoke the following sequence:

1	...	cxb2
2	Ëd1!	bxc1=♕?
3	♕xf7+!	♘xf7
4	♗xf7+	♚d8
5	♘e6	mate!

A remarkable game is **Schlechter-Nimzowitsch**, Carlsbad 1907:

1	e4	e5
2	♘f3	♘c6
3	♗b5	a6

4	♗a4	♘f6
5	♘c3	♗b4
6	♘d5	♗e7
7	0-0	0-0
8	Ëe1	d6
9	♘xf6+	♗xf6
10	c3	h6
11	h3	

One strange feature of this extraordinary game is that both players imitate their enemy's moves. 3 ♗b5 – 5 ... ♗b4; 7 0-0 0-0; 10 ... h6 – 11 h3; and there is more to come.

11	...	♘e7
12	d4	♘g6
13	♗e3	♚h7
14	♕d2	♗e6
15	♗c2	♕e7
16	d5	♗d7
17	♚h2	♘h8
18	♘g1	

Amazing. Whose nerve will be the first to crack!

18	...	g5
19	g3	♘g6
20	♕d1	♗g7
21	♕f3	a5
22	♘e2	♗b5
23	a4	♗d7

One respectable commentator called Black's last moves "a grandmasterly manoeuvre". The reader is invited to form his own judgment.

| 24 | Ëh1 | ♕e8! |

133   **W**

Watanabe-Norwood
134 World Junior Ch. 1988   **W**

25   h4?

Well, White is finally losing his patience.

25	...	♛c8!
26	♗d3	♗g4
27	♛g2	gxh4
28	f3	h3
29	♛f1	

The crux of the plan begun on his 25th move. White was now expecting 29 ... ♗d7 30 g4 followed by 31 ♛xh3 with a terrific attack.

29	...	f5!
30	fxg4	fxe4
31	♛xh3	exd3
32	♗xh6!?	♖h8!!

Black inflicts the ultimate humiliation: an echo of White's 24 ♖h1.

White resigns

The position in the above diagram was reached after the moves

1	e4	g6
2	d4	♗g7
3	♘c3	d6
4	♘f3	♘f6
5	h3	0-0
6	♗e3	a6
7	a4	b6
8	♗c4	e6

What would you feel playing against someone who puts five pawns on the sixth rank in the first eight moves? Probably a strong urge to punish the impudent fellow.

9	0-0	♗b7
10	e5	dxe5
11	♘xe5	♘bd7

(diagram 134)

Remarkably, one mistake on White's part now turns his position into a lost one.

| 12 | &f4? | ♘h5! |
| 13 | &h2 | |

13 ♘xd7? ♕xd7 14 &e5 ♕c6! ∓.

| 13 | ... | ♘xe5 |
| 14 | dxe5 | |

14 &xe5 &xe5 15 dxe5 ♕g5 is of no help.

| 14 | ... | &xe5!! |
| 15 | &xe5 | |

15 ♕xd8 &xh2+.

15	...	♕g5
16	g4	♕xe5
17	gxh5	gxh5!

Simple and effective. A deadly check is threatened at g5 (g7).

18	f4	♕c5+
19	⬜h2	♕xc4
20	♕xh5	♕d4

And **Black won**.

The game **Pomar-Petrosian**, Siegen Olympiad 1970, provided a good example of provocative opening play:

1	d4	g6
2	c4	&g7
3	♘c3	d6
4	♘f3	&g4
5	g3	♕c8!?

6	&g2	♘h6!?
7	h3	&d7
8	e4	f6

135   W

While White is playing simple and "healthy" chess, Black is developing in a most bizarre way. Since he is no patzer, it can be assumed that he is *deliberately* asking for trouble, that is he is inviting his opponent to punish such "sins" against the classical principles, in the hope (which was fulfilled in this particular game!) that White will overreach himself.

D) Implementing deception techniques in the opening

The first moves of a chess battle form a declaration of intent. Is the enemy in an attacking mood, or is he peacefully oriented? Is he interested in a theoretical duel, or is he trying to shy away from well-trodden paths? Does he have in mind a long, manoeuvring battle, or is a short, sharp skirmish on "today's menu"? The answers to these and other questions can be deduced from the information inherent in the first few moves.

Shrewd players sometimes mask their real intentions by playing certain types of openings that do not give away their intentions.

Playing a *reversed opening* (i.e. playing a Black system with the White pieces) is one possibility. GM Ludek Pachman, opening a game with 1 e4 e5 2 ♘f3 ♘c6 3 ♗e2 ♘f6 4 d3 referred to his play as "White's *seemingly* tame opening".

Later, after playing the moves c3, b3, and a3 in the first twelve moves he added: "White's *passive-looking* pieces have in reality great latent power." [67]

Such play can lead the adversary to underestimate White's position, and induce him to play too ambitiously in his desire to take advantage of it. However, reversed set-ups are perfectly playable, the attempt to "punish" them being an inappropriate response.

Other plots are also possible. Playing the aggressive Muzio Gambit with the aim of getting a better ending, or employing the sharp Sicilian Dragon with the

purpose of engaging in a purely positional contest, may prove quite confusing to the opponent.

Some opening systems certainly create false impressions. In an interesting remark to one position from his games, GM Lev Psakhis wrote: "Black's position is very solid. The main danger is that one could overestimate its possibilities." [68]

Another interesting option is to play a quiet opening that develops suddenly into a fierce combinative battle. Examples are the Colle system, or some variations of the Caro-Kann Defence, among others.

In an article entitled "Deceptive Calm", the late ex-world champion Mikhail Tal wrote:

"[Some chessplayers] are silent till the time comes, unassumingly developing pieces and apparently without serious threatening intentions. The board is dozing, the opponent is calm, and as always in similar situations, an imperceptibly prepared explosion proves extremely effective." [69]

Levenfish-Konstantinopolsky
Leningrad 1947

1	e4	c6
2	♘c3	d5
3	♘f3	dxe4

4	♘xe4	♞f6
5	♘xf6+	gxf6
6	d4	♝g4
7	♗e2	♛c7
8	c3	♞d7
9	♕a4	

This causes many problems. 9 ♗e3 was better, and if 9 ... 0-0-0 only then 10 ♕a4 ♚b8 11 0-0-0.

9	...	e6
10	♗d2	♜g8!
11	0-0-0	♝f5!
12	♜de1	

136   B

12	...	♜g4!
13	h3	♜e4

With the threat of 14 ... ♞c5! followed by 15 ... ♜xe2. We now see the drawback of White's ninth move.

14	♕b3	0-0-0
15	♗e3	c5!
16	♞d2	

White is in great difficulties: 16 ♗d3 fails to 16 ... ♜xe3! 17 ♜xe3 ♝xd3 18 ♜xd3 c4; and 16 dxc5 ♞xc5 17 ♗xc5 succumbs to 17 ... ♗h6+ 18 ♚e3 ♜xe3. These variations illustrate the power of the Black position (which arose from the modest Caro-Kann!).

16	...	cxd4!
17	♞xe4	♝xe4
18	♗d2	

Capitulation, but 18 ♗xd4 ♞c5 19 ♕c4 (19 ♗xc5 ♛xc5) 19 ... b5! does not help (20 ♕xb5 ♜xd4).

18	...	♞c5
19	♕b4	

19 ♕d1 dxc3 20 bxc3 ♛a5 is also hopeless because of the white king's shattered position.

19	...	♞d3+
20	♗xd3	♝xb4
21	♜xe4	dxc3
22	♗xc3	♜xd3
23	♜xb4	♜xc3+
	White resigns	

Portisch-Petrosian
Moscow 1967

1	d4	d5
2	c4	c6
3	cxd5	cxd5
4	♞f3	♞f6
5	♞c3	♞c6
6	♗f4	e6

7 e3   ♗d6

137   W

Most players would consider this a very boring position.

8	♗g3	0-0
9	♗d3	♖e8?!
10	♘e5	♗xe5
11	dxe5	♘d7
12	f4	♕b6?
13	0-0!	♕xe3+
14	♔h1	♕b6
15	♕h5	♘f8
16	♖f3	♘g6
17	♗f2	♕d8
18	♘b5	♘ce7
19	♘d6	♗d7
20	♗h4	♕b6
21	♖h3	h6
22	♗f6	

Quite a change from the previous diagram! White is executing a slaughter. Black has been paralysed for some moves now.

138   B

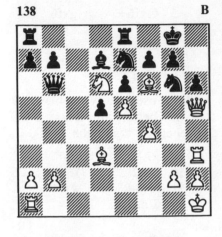

22	...	♕xb2
23	♖f1	♘f5
24	♗xf5	**Resigns**

Kurajica-Hort
139   Sombor 1968   B

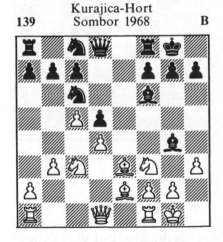

1	...	♗f5?
2	♕d2	h6
3	♖ad1	♘1e7?

GM Bojan Kurajica recalls:

"I opted for a quiet, deceptively simple line . . . Lulled into a false sense of security . . . Hort played an inferior move, after which all my pieces came to life with a vengeance . . . Caught off guard, Hort did not defend well." [70]

4	g4	♗h7
5	h4!	♘g6
6	g5	hxg5
7	hxg5	♗e7
8	♔g2	♛d7
9	♖h1	♛g4+
10	♔f1	♛e6
11	♖h2!	b6
12	♔g2	♛g4+
13	♔h1	♛e6

Black has been reduced to a very passive position.

14	♖g1	bxc5
15	dxc5	♖ad8
16	♘d4	♘xd4
17	♗xd4	f6
18	♛d3!	fxg5
19	♗g4	♛c6
20	♖e1	♘h4
21	♖xe7!	♗xd3
22	♖xg7+	♔h8
23	♖xg5+	♖f6
24	♖xh4+	Resigns

Still another ploy is to play the opening in a very peculiar way, so that the rival will not have a clue about what is going on. The British IM Michael Basman is a specialist in bizarre openings (1 ... a6; 1 ... h6). Only a few have obtained good results by following in his footsteps.

There are some other strange characters around. Take a look at this:

Hickl-I.Shrentzel
Tel Aviv 1988

1 ♘f3 ♘f6 2 g3 d6 3 ♗g2 e5 4 c4 ♗e7 5 ♘c3 c6 6 0-0 0-0 7 d3 ♘bd7 8 ♖b1 d5 9 cxd5 cxd5 10 e4!? d4 11 ♘e2 a5

Have you wondered what future White has in mind for his knight on c2?

12 ♗h3?! g6 13 ♔g2 ♖e8 14 ♘eg1!?

But of course! A manoeuvre that would cause anger and anxiety to most opponents.

Kadas-Pliester
Budapest 1985

1 h4!? e5 2 d4 exd4 3 ♘f3 ♘f6 4 c3!? dxc3 5 ♘xc3 d5 6 e4!?

Very strange . . . The fact that White won this game probably has nothing to do with the opening . . .

The author recalls a game between two young players that followed one of the silliest gambits on record: 1 e4 f5? 2 exf5 ♔f7? 3 ♛h5+ g6 4 fxg6+ ♔g7 5 gxh7 ♘f6. Apparently nowadays people have names for everything, and according to Benjamin and Schiller[71] this sequence is the "Fred" Variation, or "the Mao Tse-Tung Attack".

All I know is that when the White player saw this he laughed for quite some time, and thereafter played so badly that it was only with great effort that he saved half a point.

In the majority of cases, however, such wild experiments fail. Correct provocative play must take place within strict limits. Too much provoking can lead to disaster.

Let us sum up this chapter with the words of Znosko-Borovsky, one of the very few chess writers to have acknowledged the importance of deception in chess:

"All is for the best . . . when our combination is so forceful, or our opponent's position so weak, that we have only to go ahead without fear . . . More frequently we have to disguise our intentions, to lull our opponent to sleep, or even entice him into error. It is often necessary that he should not suspect our plans . . .

The real art consists in creating the belief, logically, that our intentions are otherwise than they seem."[72]

9 Instead of an Epilogue

It is time to sum up. I would like to repeat and emphasise some of the points that I have tried to make:

● In chess, *just as* in other games and pursuits, there are moments and situations that are dangerous, and when the wrong reaction may well lead to defeat.

● In chess, *unlike* most other sports, the dangerous moments are not always evident, and may easily be overlooked.

● It follows that guidance on how to develop a warning-system, and the systematic classification of potentially dangerous situations, may be of great use to players of all levels.

● Danger-signals may originate from various sources. The advice I have tried to give is structured around three main sources: *outside* (the opponent); *inside* (our own thought-process); and the *stimulus* itself (the board position).

● Each signal may indicate the probability that a dangerous moment is about to arrive. In practical play, several danger-signals can often be present at the same time. Thus it is vital to be able to *integrate* these signs in order to form an accurate assessment.

● A methodical search for danger is recommended. Identified dangers can be actual or potential, real or phony. The searching process does not come to a halt when a danger has been spotted. It could be that more dangers are waiting to be uncovered.

● Sensing danger is treated throughout the book as a skill that can be developed. Some techniques have been suggested, within the framework of a sustained paranoid approach.

● Finally, recognising the relevance of danger-signals has two applications: not only can we more successfully detect these signals from our own *defensive* point of view, we can also use this knowledge for *attacking* purposes. That is, we can conceal our intentions from our opponent by conscious deception.

The importance of possessing a good sense of danger cannot be exaggerated. I hope that this message has been taken, dear reader. To strengthen your alarm system, a "do you smell a rat?" quiz (in contrast to the usual "spot the winning move" tests) follows on the next few pages, to enable you to check your ability to identify dangers.

Keres-Czerniak
140   Buenos Aires 1939   **W**

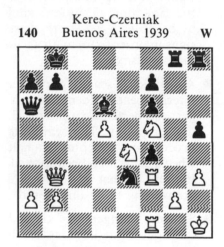

Afek-R.Lev
141   Tel Aviv 1987   **B**

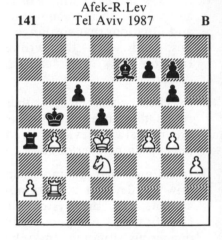

1 ♘fxd6 ♘xf1 2 ♘c5 seems to win right away (2 ... **♛b6 3 ♘d7+**). Does it?

Black played what appeared to be the natural realisation of his positional advantage: **1 ... ♝f6+ 2 ♘e5 ♜xb4+ 3 ♜xb4+ ♚xb4**. Is there something wrong in his assessment?

Rechlis-Pyernik
142 Israeli Junior Ch. 1982 **B**

Kovalsky-Blichovanetz
143 1985 **W**

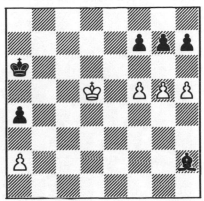

Against White's threat of 1 ♗f4 Black can choose between **1 ... ♗xb5** (1 ... ♘g6? 2 ♗xg6 wins) 2 ♗xb5+ ♘c6 3 ♕xd5 ♕d6 after which 4 ♕g5! still keeps the initiative, and **1 ... f6** intending to demonstrate that White does not have enough for his two pawns deficit.

What would you play?

We can be sure that Black knew the famous three pawns against three pawns position (1 g6! fxg6 2 h6!; or 1 .. hxg6 2 f6!). But here Black is equipped with an extra bishop!

Surely this must make a difference! Or does it not?

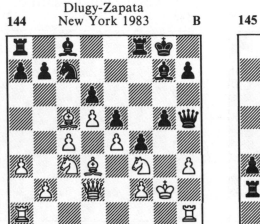

Dlugy-Zapata
New York 1983 **B**

145 Kagan-Kaldor
Israeli Ch. 1971 **B**

Black can restore material equilibrium by 1 ... dxc5. In the game he counted on **1 ... g4 2 hxg4 ♕xg4+ 3 ♔f1 ♕xf3 4 ♖h2 dxc5.**

Zapata saw that his queen was in danger, but trusted that after **5 ♗e2 ♕e3!** he would emerge from the dust a piece ahead. Was he right?

1 ... ♖a1 would have forced White's resignation in a short while. Instead, Black played the "brilliant" 1 ... ♖e2+ 2 ♔xe2 a2, oblivious to his enemy's counter-chances.

What was the snare?

A.Archakov & M.Zinar
Shakhmaty v SSSR
146 1986 **W**

White wins

White's only problem seems to be Black's d- and h-pawns. 1 &g3? h4+ or 1 &g2? h4 2 a6 h3+ are bad, but **1 &g1!** seems to do the trick. Is everything clear now, or should we search for other dangers?

Answers to Questions

1.

2 h3! wins a piece. For instance, 2 ... ♕d7 3 g4 ♘g7 4 g5.

The game concluded **2 ... cxd4 3 g4 ♕d7 4 cxd4 ♘b4 5 ♖e2** and **White won**.

2.

1 ... ♖b2? 2 ♕g6+!! fxg6 (2 ... ♕xg6 3 fxg6+ ♔xg6 4 ♗xf7+ restores material equilibrium) 3 ♗g8+ ♔h8 4 ♗b3+! draws. Likewise, 1 ... ♖c4? 2 ♕g6+!! draws in a similar fashion: 2 ... ♕xg6 3 fxg6+ ♔xg6 4 ♗c2.

By way of elimination, we must conclude that only **1 ... ♖d2!** is correct. That is the move Karpov played, and his opponent resigned at once.

3.

In the game, Black chose **5 ... ♗e6??** and after **6 exd5 ♘xd5 7 ♕f3!** he was totally lost! The game concluded **7 ... ♘xc3** (7 ... ♘c7 8 ♕xb7 ♘d7 9 ♘b5! is no better) **8 bxc3 ♘c6 9 ♖xb7 ♖c8 10 ♕xc6+! ♖xc6 11 ♗xc6+ ♗d7 12 ♖xd7 ♕g5 13 ♘f3 ♕f5 14 ♖d5+**

♔e7 **15 ♖xe5+ ♕xe5+ 16 ♘xe5 Black resigned**.

Black's faulty fifth move made White's 2 ♖b1 very handy!

4.

It is *very* wrong! **2 ... ♘f3+!!** led to a crushing defeat for White: **3 ♔h1** (3 gxf3 ♕g5+ 4 ♔h1 ♕h5) **3 ... ♕d6 4 gxf3 ♕f4 5 ♔g2 ♗h3+! 6 ♔xh3 ♕xf3+ 7 ♔h4 g5+ 8 ♔xg5 ♔h8 9 h3 ♖g8+ 10 ♔h4 ♕f6+ 11 ♔h5 ♕g5 mate**.

5.

I'm sure you saw the folly of **1 ♕f3??** g4+! **2 ♔xg4 ♗h5+!** **3 ♔xh5 ♕g5 mate**! GM Bent Larsen didn't . . .

6.

In fact, only **1 ♔h2** draws. Other moves (like **1 ♔h1??**, which occurred in the game) lose to **1 ... ♔h3!** and White will lose through zugzwang: 2 ♔g1 ♗c5+ 3 ♔h1 ♗b6 4 g4 hxg4 etc. **1 ♔h2** prevents this, for if 1 ... ♔f3 2 ♔h3! ♗xg3 stalemate.

111

7.

1 ♖c8?? (1 ♖h8+! ♔g4 2 ♖c8 draws) 1 ... ♗c3!! and one of the black pawns promotes (2 ♖xc3+ ♔g2).

8.

1 ♔d2 was correct. After White's 1 a5? Black replied strongly 1 ... ♔xb3!! 2 ♖xf3+ ♔a4! 3 ♖g3 b3 4 ♖g4+ ♔xa5 and White is helpless after both 5 ♖xg2 b2 and 5 ♔xe2 b2 6 ♖g8 ♔a6 7 ♖a8+ ♔b7. Surprisingly, it was the modest b-pawn that played the crucial role.

9.

1 f5?? would be criminal (1 ... ♕f4 mate). 1 ♗f3? was White's choice, which threw away half a point: 1 ... ♕f2+! =.
Interestingly, nor would 1 ♗e4? (1 ... ♕e3+ 2 ♗f3 ♕f2+!) or 1 ♗f7? (1 ... ♕e3+ 2 ♔h2 ♕xf4+) achieve the goal. However, 1 ♕g5+ ♔g7 2 h4! (not 2 ♗f3 ♕e1+ 3 ♔h2 ♕e3!) seems to do the trick: 2 ... h6 3 ♕g4 ♕xd5 4 h5 or 2 ... ♕e1+ 3 ♔h2 ♕xh4+ 4 ♕xh4 ♘xh4 5 ♗e4 and wins.

10.

2 ♕c3!! saves the day. The game continued 2 ... bxc3? 3 fxe7 ♕b5 4 e8=♕+ ♕xe8 5 ♗xe8 cxb2 6 ♖e1 ♘b7 7 ♘xe4 ♖xh2 and ended in a **Draw**, after White had failed to convert his advantage.

11.

The solution of No. 95 is correct, but the "solutions" of the next two diagrams contain bad errors.
In No. 96 White can win with 1 ♕h1+! ♔g6 2 ♕c6!! an idea based on a study by K.Eucken, 1947.
In No. 97 White wins by 1 ♕f8+ ♔h7 2 ♕f5!!, an idea first shown by Pogosyants, 1972.
Notice how a slight change in the position has resulted in the creation of new and brilliant ideas.

12.

In No. 111 1 ... g5! wins material: 2 ♗g3 g4 3 ♘g1 ♗xg2. That is how the game Nurnberg-Rodl, Riedenburg 1947, ended.

13.

The second variation is correct, though it should be carried on a little further: 5 ♔f3 ♔d3 6 ♔f2 (6 a4 c4 7 a5 c3 8 a6 c2 9 a7 c1=♕ 10 a8=♕ ♕h1+) 6 ... c4 7 ♔e1 ♔c2! 8 a4 c3 and wins.
The first one contains a serious flaw: 1 ... ♔c8? 2 ♖e7 ♔d8 3 ♖e6!! ♔d7 4 ♖e5! ♘d3+ 5 ♔e3! ♘xe5 6 ♘xc5+ drawing.

14.

The worst possibility lies in the variation 1 ... a6?? 2 ♖e5!! as actually happened in the game. Mate is unavoidable.

Answers to "Do You Smell a Rat?" Quiz

140.

According to Czerniak,[73] Keres was in serious time trouble. He wrote 1 ♘fxd6 on his score-sheet but then changed his mind and played another move.

The intended 1 ♘fxd6? ♘xf1 2 ♘c5 would fail to 2 ... ♘g3+! and here the various continuations are in Black's favour: 3 ♖xg3? ♕f1+; or 3 ♔g1 ♕b6!; or 3 ♔h2 ♘f1+ 4 ♖xf1? (4 ♔g1? ♖xg2+!, but he can draw by repetition with 4 ♔h1) 4 ... ♖xg2+! 5 ♔xg2 ♕e2+, winning.

Keres probably felt that 1 ♘fxd6 was too good to be true, and played the strong 1 ♘xe3! fxe3 2 ♕xe3 ♗e5 3 ♘xf6 ♗xf6 4 ♖xf6 ♕xa2 5 ♕e5+ ♔a8 6 ♖xf7. The rest of the game is noteworthy if only because of its aesthetic "finale": 6 ... ♕c4 7 b3 ♕c2 (7 ... ♕xb3? 8 ♕xh8) 8 ♖1f2 ♕c5 9 ♕e7 ♕xe7 10 ♖xe7 ♖d8 11 ♖f5 h4 12 ♔g1 ♖c8 13 d6 ♖c1+ 14 ♔h2 ♖d1 15 d7 ♖d8 16 ♖e8 ♖1xd7 17 ♖ff8! **Black resigned**.

141.

He was dead wrong. 1 ... ♗f6+ 2 ♘e5 ♖xb4+?? 3 ♖xb4+ ♔xb4 4 g5! led to Black's immediate resignation!

The reason is that in the ensuing pawn ending White will create a passed pawn on the king's flank: 4 ... ♗xe5+ (forced) 5 fxe5 with the plan 6 h4 followed by 7 h5 gxh5 8 g6!. Black is helpless: 5 ... c5+ 6 ♔xd5 c4 7 ♔d4 c3 8 ♔d3 ♔c5 9 e6 fxe6 10 ♔xc3 ±±.

Had he been suspicious, Black could have kept his winning chances with 2 ... ♗xe5+ 3 fxe5 g5!.

142.

1 ... f6?? led to a quick finish. Black did not sense the clouds that had gathered around his undeveloped position:

2 ♖xe6!! ♗xe6 3 ♗f4 ♕d8 4 ♗c7!

Pretty and original. Either the king or queen has to go. **White won**.

113

143.

Yes, it does make a difference. Being alert and careful does not mean that we should be afraid of ghosts!

1 g6 hxg6! 2 f6 ♗e5! led to Black's victory: **3 ♔xe5 gxf6+** with **4 ... gxh5.**

144.

This is a case of one danger making the player blind to the other possible dangers in the position. It is true that after **5 ... ♛e3!** the queen is *temporarily* saved, but in the long run the queen cannot find a safe haven: **6 ♛c2! ♛d4 7 f3!** (7 ♖d1? f3! ∓) **7 ... b5 8 ♖d1 bxc4 9 d6! ♘e6 10 ♘b5 ♛e3 11 ♛xc4 ♔h8 12 ♖d3** (finally capturing the imprisoned lady) **12 ... ♘g5 13 ♖xe3 fxe3 14 ♔g2** and Black's further resistance did not change the obvious outcome. **White won.**

145.

White had an undeserved lucky escape: **3 ♖h6+! ♔e5 4 ♖h5+ Draw** since Black dare not play 4 ... ♔f4?? 5 ♖f5+ and 6 ♖f1, nor 4 ... ♔d4?? 5 ♔d2! a1=♛ 6 ♖d5 mate, nor 4 ... ♔e6 5 ♖h6+ ♔e7?? 6 ♖h7+ and 7 ♖a7. Black missed victory because he did not bother to look for his enemy's possible replies. Let that be a lesson for us all!

146.

It is not over yet. **1 ♔g1! d3 2 ♔f1!!** (2 ♔f2 g5!! 3 a6 g4 4 a7 g3+; the far-away g-pawn can be a source of trouble!).

If **1 ... c4 2 ♔f1 c3** then only **3 ♔e1!** assures the victory: 3 ♔e2? f5!! 4 a6 f4 5 a7 f3+ and we realise that the f-pawn could also prove to be a menace.

Bibliographical References

1. Kotov, A. in Krogius, N., *Psychology in Chess*, RHM Press, New York 1976, p.48.
2. Koontz, H. & Bradspies, R.W., "Managing Through Feedforward Control" in *Business Horizons* 6/72, pp.25-36.
3. Krogius, N., op. cit., p.48.
4. Mednis, E., *How to Beat Bobby Fischer*, Quadrangle, New York 1974, p.177.
5. Littlewood, J., *Chess Coaching*, Crowood 1991, p.52.
6. Dvoretsky, M., "The Feeling for Danger" in *New in Chess* 8/85, p.44.
7. Kotov, A., *Think Like a Grandmaster*, Batsford, London 1975, p.62.
8. Czerniak, M., *XVI Chess Olympiad*, Israel Chess Federation 1966, p.145.
9. Porath, J. in *Shahmat* 12/66, p.303 (in Hebrew).
10. Kasparov, G., *The Test of Time*, Pergamon 1986, p.46.
11. Alburt, L., *Test and Improve Your Chess*, Pergamon 1989, p.26.
12. Mednis, E., *From the Middlegame into the Endgame*, Pergamon 1987, p.9.
13. Benko, P., *Winning with Chess Psychology*, McKay, New York 1991, p.218.
14. Greenfeld, A., interview in *Chess in Israel* 4/90, p.29 (in Hebrew).
15. Benko, P., op. cit., p.71.
16. Bushinsky, S. in *Chess in Israel* 12/91, p.52 (in Hebrew).
17. Kashdan, I. (ed.), *Second Piatigorsky Cup*, Dover, New York 1968, p.97-98.
18. Karpov, A. & Roshal, A., *Chess is My Life*, Pergamon 1980, p.87.
19. Krogius, N., op. cit., p.30.
20. Chernev, I., *Capablanca's Best Chess Endings*, Dover, New York 1982, p.240.
21. Makarichev, S., "How We Almost Lost the European Championship" in *New in Chess* 1/90, p.56.
22. Pachman, L., *Decisive Games in Chess History*, Dover, New York 1987, p.22.
23. Dvoretsky, M., "Beyond Theory" in *New in Chess* 4/91, p.80.
24. Pein, M. in *Shahmat* 2-3/1989, p.79 (in Hebrew).
25. Schmidt, P., *How Chessmasters Think*, Chess Enterprises, USA 1989, p.79.
26. Webb, S., *Chess for Tigers*, Maxwell Macmillan 1990, p.66.
27. Flear, G., "Why is He Playing On?" in *Chess* 9/88, p.7.
28. Dvoretsky, M., *Secrets of Chess Training*, Batsford, London 1991, p.16.
29. Krabbe, T., *Chess Curiosities*, George Allen & Unwin 1985, p.89.
30. Short, N., interview in *New in Chess* 2/86, p.39.

31. Hartston, W.R. & Wason, P.C., *The Psychology of Chess*, Batsford, London 1983, p.88.
32. Malkin, V.B., "Problems Associated with the Chessplayer's Psychological Preparation" in Estrin, Y. & Romanov, I (ed.), *The World Champions Teach Chess*, A & C Black, London 1988, p.201.
33. Psakhis, L. in *Chess in Israel* 7/91, p.61 (in Hebrew).
34. Polugayevsky, L., *Grandmaster Performance*, Pergamon 1984, p.152.
35. De Groot, A., *Thought and Choice in Chess*, Mouton 1978, p.261.
36. Vasiliev, V.L., *Tigran Petrosian, His Life and Games*, Batsford, London 1974, p.230.
37. Hartston, W.R. & Wason, P.C., op. cit., p.96.
38. Miles, A.J. in *Chess* 4/76, pp.209-210.
39. Schweitzer, D., "A Monologue of a Coach" in *Leadership* 6/90, p.49 (in Hebrew).
40. Romanovsky, P., *Izbranie Partie*, Moscow 1954, pp.52-55 (in Russian).
41. Taylor in Cockborn, A., *Idle Passion: Chess and the Dance of Death*, New American Library, USA, p.134.
42. Hartston, W.R. & Wason, P.C., op. cit., p.92.
43. Salov, V., interview in *New in Chess* 4/91, p.63.
44. Avni, A., Kipper, D.A. & Fox, S., "Personality and Leisure Activities: An Illustration with Chessplayers" in *Journal of Personality & Individual Differences* 1987, pp.715-719.
45. Petrosian, T. in *The World Champions Teach Chess*, op. cit., p.123.
46. Norwood, D. in *Chess* 10/91, pp.24-25.
47. Krogius, N., op. cit., p.75.
48. Soltis, A., *Catalog of Chess Mistakes*, McKay, New York 1979, p.30.
49. Dvoretsky, M., op. cit. (*NIC* 1991), p.80.
50. Williams, R.W., "Surprise, the Danger Signals" in *Army* 4/74, p.13.
51. Soltis, A., op. cit., p.15.
52. Littlewood, J., op. cit., p.57.
53. Alburt, L & Parr, L., "Strongpoints: The Dvoretsky Method" in *Chess Life* 11/91, pp.740-742.
54. Dvoretsky, M., op. cit. (Batsford 1991), p.148.
55. Grabo, C.M., *Warning Intelligence*, Virginia 1987, pp.20-21.
56. Hearst, E. & Wierzbicki, M., "Battle Royal: Psychology and the Chessplayer" in Goldstean (ed.), *Sports, Games & Play*, Erlbaum 1979, pp.59-60.
57. Webb, S., op. cit., p.55.
58. Krogius, N., op. cit., p.174.
59. Shereshevsky, M.I., *Endgame Strategy*, Pergamon 1988, pp.45-46.
60. Krogius, N., op. cit., p.174.
61. Karpov, A. & Roshal, A., op. cit., p.221.
62. Nikitin, A. in Zak, V., *Improve Your Chess Results*, Batsford, London 1985, p.191.

63. Kagan, S in *Shahmat* 1/78, p.18 (in Hebrew).
64. Kaplan, J., "Games from Lone Pine" in *Chess Life* 7/77, p.366.
65. Botvinnik, M.M. in Hartston, W.R. & Wason, P.C., op. cit., p.95.
66. Botvinnik, M.M., *Achieving the Aim*, Pergamon 1981, p.165.
67. Pachman, L., *Complete Chess Strategy (2)*, Batsford, London 1976, pp. 154-155.
68. Psakhis, L. in *Chess in Israel* 10/91, p.18 (in Hebrew).
69. Tal, M in *Shahmaty Riga* 3/66, p.13 (in Russian).
70. Kurajica, B. in Keene, R.D. (ed), *Learn from the Grandmasters*, McKay, USA 1975, p.52.
71. Benjamin, J & Schiller, E., *Unorthodox Openings*, Batsford, London 1987, p.87.
72. Znosko-Borovksy, E., *The Art of Chess Combinations*, Dover, New York 1959, p.181.
73. Czerniak, M., *The Book of Chess*, Mass, Jerusalem 1967, p.117 (in Hebrew).

Index of Players

(references are to diagram numbers)